CHRISTIANITY'S JEWISH HERITAGE

The Church of the Circumcision

The Church of the Gentiles

Christianity's Jewish Heritage

Sr. BRIGID YOUNGHUGHES SHCJ

Angel Press

First published in 1988 by Angel Press
P.O. Box 60, East Wittering, West Sussex PO20 8RA

© Brigid Younghughes SHCJ, 1988

British Library Cataloguing in Publication Data

Younghughes, Brigid. *1908 –*
    Christianity's Jewish heritage
    1. Judaism — For Christians.
    I. Title
    296

ISBN 0 – 947785 – 26 – 4

Typeset in Times by Woodfield Graphics, Fontwell, West Sussex.
Printed in Great Britain by Hollen Street Press Ltd. at Slough, Berkshire

Contents

Acknowledgements

I have taken the English Bible quotations from the Revised Version, since this is a well-known translation which keeps very close to the original Hebrew and Greek. The quotations from the Apocrypha I have taken from the Authorised Version.

I should like to thank Mrs Ann Plumptre and Mr Guy Wickenden of IEF, and Dr Ann Saddlemeyer of the University of Toronto, without whose faith and encouragement this book would never have been completed. Also, my thanks to Mrs Penny Faust of CCJ, whose kindly and uninhibited criticism of the first draft led me to read more widely and to alter the whole form of presentation to its considerable advantage.

Introduction

At the Annual Conference of The International Ecumenical Fellowship, held at Bovendonk in Holland in August 1986 we took as our theme these words of Jesus, 'I have come not to abolish but to fulfil,' and sought by prayer, discussion, lectures, music and art to discover the ideals and practices we share with, and have often inherited from these our brethren.

The members of our working party were astonished to discover how much Christianity has inherited from her Jewish roots, and how much the example of Jewish life and worship has to share with us. They thought it sad that many sincere Christians were still as ignorant of these riches as they had been before coming to the conference, and thought that there was need for a simple outline of our shared heritage, so that all Christians could appreciate for themselves how much we owe to Judaism and how much we each have to give the other. This book is an attempt to meet such a need. It is not meant to be a learned thesis on the subject: such books already abound and are well worth attention by the student of Jewish/Christian religion, life and literature. But not everyone has time or inclination for such study. This booklet is intended for the average, intelligent person who is interested in the roots of Christianity and who will appreciate going back to its origins.

If this taste of the subject should lead any reader to further study it would be a bonus, but if it should simply lead to those who read it acquiring an increased understanding of, and a greater openness towards our Jewish heritage, it will have achieved its purpose.

Preface

It is increasingly common nowadays to remind ourselves that Jesus was a Jew, born and brought up in the Law of Moses, that he respected this law and taught his followers to do so. He regularly attended the synagogue and the great feasts in the temple: we see him doing this in all four Gospels. He taught, healed and did other good works among his own people and when he sent his disciples out on a preaching tour he instructed them:

> Go not into any way of the Gentiles, and enter not into any city of the Samaritans:
> But go ye rather to the lost sheep of the house of Israel.
>
> (Matthew X.5f)

It is well that we have come to realize, even so belatedly, that our Jewish brethren are our elder brothers.

But perhaps it is not always so clearly realized that all Jesus' apostles and early followers were Jews, saturated from birth in the religion and tradition of their race; so how could they fail to bring with them into the early Christian Church the very strongest flavour of Jewish life, religion and morality. The first Christian churches were known as synagogues, although this is obscured by the usual English translation of James II.2: 'If there come unto your synagogue' (*eistin synagogin* in the original Greek) but usually rendered (quite correctly) as 'your assembly' in English.

Into these Christian synagogues came Jews, Palestinian Jews and Diaspora Jews (like Stephen) and also Proselytes and God fearers, Gentiles who had accepted Judaism or who were very near to the Jewish faith, but who had not yet embraced it fully by accepting circumcision.

Judaism in the time of Jesus was composed of many sects who, acknowledging Yahweh, the One God, interpreted his Torah in varied ways. We know of: Pharisees, Sadducees, Hasidim, Zealots, Sicarii, Essenes, The Qumran Community, the community for which the Damascus Document was written, Jewish

2

Gnostics, Hellenes, Baptizing Sects (including that of John the Baptist) Healing Sects, etc. etc. Christianity was at first looked on as merely another variation of Jadaism. Jesus' teaching in no way contravened the written Torah, in fact it made it stricter and freed it only from restrictions in the 'oral Torah' (i.e. the traditions handed down by word of mouth) by emphasizing the importance of the written scriptures:

> Why do thy disciples transgress the traditions of the elders? For they wash not their hands when they eat bread.
>
> And he answered and said unto them, Why do ye also transgress the commandments of God because of your tradition?
>
> For God said, Honour thy father and thy mother: and he that speaketh evil of father or mother, let him die the death.
>
> But ye say, Whosoever shall say to his father or his mother, that wherewith thou mightest have been profited by me is given to God;
>
> He shall not honour his father. And ye have made void the word of God because of your tradition.
>
> (Matthew XV.2ff)

After the destruction of the Temple in A.D.70 Palestinian Judaism would have been left comparatively rudderless, had not Rabbi Johanan ben Zakkai and his fellow scholars set up the Rabbinic Academy at Jamnia (Javne) from where they codified the oral law, in the Mishnah, towards the end of the second century A.D. and declared the 'minim' (heretics, including Christians) anathema in the twelfth benediction of the Amidah Prayer. Although not written down until late second century the Mishnah undoubtedly embodies material at least from the time of Ezra and is largely characteristic of practice in New Testament times, although we cannot be sure just how much some details may have been 'tidied up' before being committed to writing. It is our main source for Pharisaic Judaism as Jesus and his disciples, and the early Christians of the first century must have known it. We can gain some facts, too, from St. Paul's epistles, written largely between 50 and 60 A.D. The gospels are even later, being written, except for Mark, after the fall of Jerusalem and all four outside Palestine. Scholars are agreed that, although they relate events which happened in the first three decades of the century, their atmosphere is heavily impregnated by the relations between Christians and Jews towards the end of the century, i.e. around the time of the condemnation of Christianity at Jamnia. The other New Testament writings fall into much the same space of time: 2 Peter, probably the latest, being dated by most scholars in the early second century.

We can, however, be reasonably sure that Jesus and his followers must have recited the Shema twice daily, evening and morning, and have recited the Amidah Prayer at every Temple or synagogue service, and the first Christians must surely have brought back to their Christian synagogues the way of worship and the way of life which had been theirs from childhood. And it would seem that this Church, composed of Jews who had accepted Christianity but who still kept the Mosaic Law, was still in existence in the fifth century: a century after the acceptance of Christianity by the Roman Empire.

Apart from heresies there were, too, disputes on matters of Law and Ritual, even between leading rabbis within the sect of the Pharisees themselves, and the opinions of some of the leading disputants are preserved in the Mishnah. Especially important for our purpose are those which took place early in the first century A.D. between the powerful Rabbis Hillel and Shammai, near- contemporaries of Jesus. Very likely, as a boy of twelve, he heard these two great authorities argue in the temple courts, where his parents found him:

> Sitting in the midst of the doctors, both hearing them and asking them questions.
>
> (Luke II.46)

Their disputes and those of their disciples can help us to recreate the religious atmosphere in Jerusalem during the so- called inter- testamental period. Then, as we know from the great amount of apocalyptic and eschatological literature being produced, religious ideas were in ferment as probably never before.

I propose to set the scene with a brief resumé of Judean history between the destruction of Jerusalem by Nebuchadnessar and the Babylonian Exile to its destruction again by Titus and the establishment of the Rabbinic Academy at Jamnia: i.e. from the

4

end of the sixth century B.C. to the end of the first century A.D. The first six hundred years are necessary to enable us to visualize Judaism at the time of Jesus, hardened and disciplined by conquest and exile but still pliant and open (too open many complained) to influences from outside. The last decade, and especially the last thirty years of this decade, will allow us to see it setting into a mold canonized for ever in the Mishnah, which we can recognize as the Judaism we know today.

Then I will try to estimate what we may be reasonably sure the early Christian Church inherited from her parent, Judaism, and which, with the Christian Scriptures, has formed the foundation which she now hands on to us, her children. A brief summary of sources will show where further study may lead.

1. The Situation

> And when they perceived the grace which was given unto me,
> James and Cephas and John, they who were reputed to be pillars,
> gave to me and Barnabas the right hand of fellowhip, that we should
> go to the Gentiles and they to the Circumcision.
>
> (Galatians II.9)

In these words, in his letter to the Galatian Christians in the
fifties of the first century, St. Paul records the agreement made
by the leaders of the Christian Church at Jerusalem concerning the
evangelization of Jews and pagans. St. Paul taught that Jews who
became Christians were still bound by obedience to the Jewish Law,
which Jesus himself and his apostles had observed. Paul made this
clear when he 'took and circumcised Timothy, the son of a Jewess
who believed' (Acts XVI. 1 to 3) since, according to Jewish law
a child of a Jewish mother, although his father be a Gentile, is a
Jew; whereas the child of a Gentile mother, although his father be a
Jew, is not accepted as a Jew by birth but must, should he so wish,
become one by conversion; this is still the law. Equally firmly, Paul
taught that converts from among the Gentiles were bound only by
what is known as the Noachic Covenant, which the Jews held to
be what God had demanded from the sons of Noah (before the
full law was given on Sinai) and which remained binding on all
mankind: to abstain from idolatry, bloodshed, fornication, theft,
to establish a just administration and to slaughter animals properly,
without unecessary cruelty and without leaving 'the blood in them,'
since it was believed that 'the blood is the life' and life belongs to
God alone. (Without this last requirement there could have been
no table-fellowship between Jewish and Gentile converts in the
infant Church.)

That these two branches of the Church existed side by side
as late as the fifth century is shown by an early mosaic in the
Church of Sancta Sabina in Rome, where two Roman matrons, one
called 'Ecclesia Circumcisione' and the other 'Ecclesia Gentibus'
stand one on each side of the central mosaic bearing the words of

dedication of the Church, and this mosaic tells us that the church was built during the reign of Pope Celestine (i.e. Celestine I, 422 to 432 A.D.) But that there was danger of friction between the two branches of the nascent Church makes itself evident from the beginning:

> Now in these days, when the number of the disciples was multiplying, there arose a murmuring of the Grecian Jews (i.e. those from the Diaspora) against the Hebrews, because their widows were neglected in the daily ministration.
>
> (Acts. VI.1)

This complaint was dealt with by the appointment of deacons who, from their names, seem to have been chosen from the 'Greek' party. These early differences were between Jews converted to Christianity and inevitably friction increased when converts from among the Gentiles were admitted to the Church; this is clear from St. Paul's epistles, especially that to the Galatians. It appears that the 'Church of the Circumcision' regarded the concession to the converted Gentiles, to be bound by the Noachic Covenant only and not to be forced to abide by the full Law of Moses, as a temporary expedient which would in due course be superseded by the converts' acceptance of the full Law of Moses:

> Except ye be circumcised after the custom of Moses ye cannot be saved.
>
> (Acts XV.1)

Whereas St. Paul and his fellow missionaries taught that the concession was for all time:

> Christ redeemed us from the curse of the law (i.e. from being accursed, unable to be saved, unless you obey the law) that upon the Gentiles might come the blessing of Christ Jesus: that they might receive the promise of the Spirit through faith.
>
> (Galatians III.13 ff.)

We know very little of the subsequent history of the 'Church of the Circumcision', but its position must have become increasingly difficult after the Fall of Jerusalem and the destruction of the temple in A.D.70 and even more so after the condemnation of the Christian 'heresy' at the Synod of Jamnia (Javne) in about A.D.88. Its members seem to have been absorbed by the 'Church of the Gentiles' or to have faded from Christian history among the numerous gnostic sects of the first five centuries of the Christian era. There is no denying that the Gentile Church became increasingly estranged from its Jewish origins, especially after the recognition of Christianity by the Roman Emperor Constantine early in the fourth century. Christians, with their often only nominally-Christian governments, persecuted the Jews throughout the next fifteen centuries, until hatred culminated in the horrors of the Holocaust. The knowledge that such acts can be performed in the name of Christianity has profoundly shocked all sincere Christians and forced us to examine our consciences, to try to understand how such things could have been perpetrated by a people who trace their religious roots to Jesus of Nazareth, who was a Jew by birth, upbringing and in his way of life and who taught us:

Salvation is of the Jews. (John IV.22)

and:

Think not that I came to destroy the law or the prophets: I came not to destroy, but to fulfil.

(Matthew V.17)

And surely 'to fulfil' means to complete, in the sense of bringing to perfection, not, as Christians have all too often interpreted it, to render obsolete; to fulfil in such a way as to perfect a foundation on which to build further.
Thanks be to God that this is being increasingly appreciated and that Christians today are seeking to find their way back to their Jewish roots, and to love and fellowship with their Jewish brethren.

2. Brief Historical Resumé

Between 597 and 587 B.C. Jerusalem and the temple had been destroyed and the cream of the people carried off to Babylon; in about 520 B.C. the Persians, having conquered Babylon, allowed those exiles who wished to return to Judea under the governor Zerubabel and the priest Joshua ben Jehozadek.

From 539 to 323 was a time of Persian domination; this is the period covering the work of the prophets Ezra and Nehemiah.

In 323, Alexander the Great conquered the Persians and Judea was subject to his successors until the outbreak of the Maccabean Revolt.

During this period the Psalms were probably collected, though many of them date from much earlier, and they became the 'hymn book' of the temple, belatedly restored by the returned exiles (See the prophets Haggai and Zechariah). About this time, too, I and II Chronicles and Ecclesiastes were written, and the three pilgrim feasts: (Unleavened Bread, in the Spring, Shavuot or Weeks, or Pentecost, in the late Spring and Succoth, or Booths, or Tabernacles in the autumn) were declared to be times when every male must present himself before the Lord, and these occasions drew Jews not only from Palestine, but from the whole Diaspora to Jerusalem.

The Pentateuch (also called the Torah) was probably compiled around 450 B.C. and rose rapidly to authoritative eminence; we know that it was read in the temple and that it was acknowledged as authoritative by the Samaritans as well as the Jews, for when the Samaritans separated from the Jews, finally, in the time of Nehemiah about the middle of the fifth century they took their own copy of the Pentateuch with them. Nehemiah tells us that Ezra read 'the book' and that individuals helped the people to understand; perhaps this means that they translated it from Hebrew to Aramaic, which had become the vernacular, although Hebrew remained the language of the liturgy. So as early as the time of Ezra, around 390, perhaps earlier, there existed public reading and explanation, perhaps including translation of the Torah. In around 250 B.C. it

9

was translated into Greek, in the translation which we know as the Septuagint (LXX): the Bible of the early Church.

Up to the time of the Greeks the conquerors of Palestine had been interested in acquiring land and political advantages, but had not interfered with religion. The Greeks, however, sought to bring to the conquered people their language, customs and institutions. After 198 B.C., Palestine belonged to the Syrian Greeks and Antiochus IV, Ephiphanes, sought to tempt or force the Jews from their religious obedience; in 168 he desecrated the temple by replacing Yahweh's altar of holocausts by one dedicated to Zeus, to whom he sacrificed swine.

The persecution of the Jews, and the desecration of the temple by Antiochus led to the Maccabean revolt and to the establishment of a precarious Jewish autonomy under the Hasmonean dynasty, from 100 to 40 B.C. After a brief interval Herod the Great, who was only partly Jewish, took the throne and reigned from 37 to 4 B.C. On his death Palestine was divided among his sons: Archelaeus was appointed to rule Judea, but was deposed, after Jewish complaints, in A.D.6.; Herod Antipas became Tetrarch of Galilee, which he held until A.D.39.; Philip became Tetrarch of North Trans-Jordan.

From A.D.6 to 66 Judea was ruled by Roman procurators, of whom Pontius Pilate ruled from 26 to 36 A.D. In A.D. 37 Caligula appointed Herod Agrippa, a grandson of Herod the Great, King of Judea. In A.D.39 Herod Antipas was deposed in Galilee and Herod Agrippa became ruler of all that Herod the Great had held. On his death in A.D.44 Judea reverted to the rule of Roman procurators. But the procurator Florus, who ruled from 64 to 66 plundered the land and desecrated the temple and in 66 revolt again broke out. In 68 Vespasian arrived to deal with this and, on his appointment as Emperor in 69 his son Titus took command. The Romans decided that they had been tolerant long enough with these people, the Jews. In 70 Titus destroyed Jerusalem and carried away the temple treasure and in 73 he conquered the last Jewish stronghold at Masada; rebellion was at an end.

But the rabbis set up a school at Jamnia, where the synod replaced the Great Sanhedrin, and from A.D. 90 this became the centre of religious affairs; the rabbis assembled there set to work to reform, refine, re-unite a Judaism deeply wounded by the destruction of Jerusalem and the temple.

These events, from the time of Herod the Great, are behind the New Testament period and frequently reflected in Christian writings. During this time Christianity spread throughout the known world; she produced her own scriptures and from the end of the first century went increasingly her own way.

Her salvation lay in the fact that, unlike the Essenes or the Qumran Community, she had not repudiated rabbinic Judaism, but had continued to attend the temple as long as it was standing, and the worship of her synagogues was similar to that held in all other Jewish synagogues throughout Jerusalem, Palestine and the Diaspora. This meant that when the time came, towards the end of the century, that rabbinic Jadaism repudiated the Christian 'heresy' the new sect was strong enough and pliant enough to stand on her own.

3. The Jewish Family

From the earliest documents we have the Israelite family has always been patriarchal; the husband is *ba'al*, lord, of his family, consisting of wives, children and slaves, and this included married sons and their wives, if they lived at home. But by New Testament times urban life had necessitated a decrease in numbers and a son at marriage was often said to 'build himself a house.' However sons did continue to live at home, viz. those in the parable of The Prodigal Son (Luke XV.11) We are not told whether the sons were married but it would not have made any difference so long as they both stayed and worked for their father. St. Paul compares the life of an heir before he comes of age to that of a slave.

The nearest male relative, if there was no son to succeed, was the father's brother (Lev. XXV.49) and members of the family in a wide sense had the duty to protect one another. If a man fell into slavery he should be redeemed:

> And if thy brother be waxen poor, and his hand fail with thee; then thou shalt uphold him: as a stranger and a sojourner shall he live with thee.

> Take thou no usury of him nor increase...

> And if thy brother be waxen poor with thee, and sell himself unto thee; thou shalt not make him to serve as a bondservant...

> And if a stranger or sojourner with thee be waxen rich, and thy brother be waxen poor beside him, and sell himself unto the stranger or sojourner with thee...

> After that he is sold he may be redeemed; one of his brethren may redeem him:

> Or his uncle, or his uncle's son, or any that is nigh of kin unto him of his family may redeem him.
>
> (Leviticus XXV.35,36,47 to 49)

Similarly if he had to sell his patrimony his 'family' should redeem it, his brother, then his uncle or uncle's son, then any relative; this

12

practice is behind the scene in the book of Jeremiah when Jeremiah's uncle's son came to him in besieged Jerusalem saying:

> Buy my field, I pray thee, that is in Anathoth: for the right of redemption is thine to buy it...
> And I bought the field that was in Anathoth...
>
> (Jeremiah XXXII.7,9)

This close-knit sense of the family has never left the Jews. At the end of the last century, and the beginning of this when they were fleeing from the pogroms in Europe, Jewish communities would welcome newcomers in so far as they were able, and help to set even distant relatives on their feet when they arrived, often penniless. This sense of family the Jew of today still retains, and here, as in all matters pertaining to the family, he has much to teach us and share with us.

Trades were probably often handed down from father to son; it was a father's duty to teach his son the duties of religion:

> ...Take heed to thyself, and keep thy soul diligently, lest thou forget the things which thine eye saw, and lest thou depart from thy heart all the days of thy life; but make them known unto thy children and thy children's children.
>
> (Deuteronomy XXXII.7)

and also to teach him a trade. The rabbis taught that a man who did not teach his son an honest trade was bringing him up to be a thief. Even Paul of Tarsus, sent by his pious family to study at the feet of Gamaliel in Jerusalem, had been taught a trade before he left home, so that later in Corinth he was able to earn his living at it and remain independent from the charity of his somewhat unpredictable Corinthian converts:

> And he found a certain Jew named Aquila, a man of Pontus by race, lately come from Italy, with his wife Priscilla...and he came unto them;
> And because he was of the same trade, he abode with them, and they wrought; for by trade they were tent makers.
>
> (Acts. XVIII.2,3)

Jesus of course was a carpenter, son of a carpenter:

13

And when the sabbath was come, he began to teach in the synagogue: and many hearing him were astonished, saying, 'Whence has this man these things, and, what is the wisdom that is given unto this man, and what mean such mighty works wrought by his hands?'

'Is not this the carpenter, the son of Mary, and brother of James, and Joses, and Judas, and Simon?'

(Mark VI.2,3)

And coming into his own country he taught them in their synagogue, insomuch as they were astonished, and said, 'Whence has this man this wisdom, and these mighty works?

Is not this the carpenter's son? is not his mother called Mary? and his brethren, James, and Joseph, and Simon, and Judas?'

(Matthew XIII.54ff)

MARRIAGE: POLYGAMY OR MONOGAMY

Genesis II. 21 to 24 presents monogamous marriage as the will of God:

And the man said, 'This is now bone of my bones, and flesh of my flesh...'

Therefore shall a man leave his father and mother, and shall cleave unto his wife: and they shall be one flesh.

(vv. 23 and 24)

Polygamy does not appear until Lamak, of the reprobate line of Cain, takes two wives (Genesis IV.19). According to the Code of Hammurabi (c. 1700 B.C.) a husband may not take a second wife unless the first is barren and he loses this right if the wife herself gives him a slave as concubine, or as Sarai did to Abram, as a wife:

And Sarai Abram's wife took Hagar the Egyptian, her handmaid, after Abram had dwelt twelve years in the land of Canaan, and gave her to Abram her husband to be his wife.

(Genesis XVI.3)

The husband could of course always take a concubine, even if he had children by his wife, but her children never had the same rights as those of a wife and he might not take a second concubine unless the first was barren. But these rules were not always observed and Deuteronomy XXI 15 to 17 recognizes the right to bigamy, taking

14

steps to ensure that the eldest son receives his rights in spite of his father's preference, perhaps, for the son of his old age, and of his young wife:

> If a man have two wives, the one beloved, and the other hated, and they have borne him children, both the beloved and the hated; and if the firstborn son be hers that was hated;
>
> Then it shall be, in the day that he causeth his sons to inherit that which he hath, that he may not make the son of the beloved the firstborn before the son of the hated, which is the firstborn:
>
> But he shall acknowledge the firstborn, the son of the hated, by giving him a double portion of all that he hath: for he is the beginning of his strength; the right of the firstborn is his.
>
> (Deuteronomy XXI.15 to 17)

Later the oral law fixed the limit at four wives for subjects, eighteen for kings. But in fact few men could afford more than one and monogomy was practised throughout Israel long before New Testament times. In spite of deviations, it has indeed always been the preferred form of marriage in Israel; the prophets are fond of showing Israel as the one wife chosen by the One God:

> Thus saith the Lord, 'I remember for thee the kindness of thy youth, the love of thine espousals; how thou wentest after me in the wilderness...'
>
> (Jeremiah II.2)

> Thus saith the Lord, 'Where is the bill of your mother's divorcement, wherewith I have put her away? Or which of my creditors is it to whom I have sold you?'
>
> (Isaiah L.1)

and the Wisdom Literature delights to praise the worth of a good wife:

> A virtuous woman who can find? for her price is far above rubies.
>
> The heart of her husband trusteth in her, and he shall have no lack of gain.
>
> She does him good and not evil all the days of her life.
>
> She seeketh wool and flax, and worketh willingly with her hands...

She spreadeth out her hand to the poor; yea she reacheth forth her hand to the needy.

She is not afraid of the snow for her household; for all her household are clothed with scarlet, (or perhaps 'are doubly clothed')

Her husband is known in the gates, when he sitteth among the elders of the land...

She openeth her mouth with wisdom; and the law of kindness is upon her tongue.

She looketh well to the ways of her household, and eateth not the bread of idleness.

Her children rise up and call her blessed; her husband also, and he praiseth her, saying:

Many daughters have done virtuously, but thou excelleth them all.

Favour is deceitful, and beauty is vain: but a woman that feareth the LORD, she shall be praised.

(Proverbs XXXI.10 ff)

THE ISRAELITE MARRIAGE

The married woman was totally under her husband's authority, as the unmarried girl was under her father's. The decalogue lists her among his possessions:

Thou shalt not covet thy neighbour's house, thou shalt not covet thy neighbour's wife, nor his manservant, nor his maidservant, nor his ox, nor his ass, nor any thing that is thy neighbour's.

(Exodus XX.17)

The bridegroom paid a sum of money the *mohar* to his wife's father, but this was not a purchase-price; the father had only the usufruct of it and it reverted to his daughter when she succeeded or if her husband reduced her to penury. Bridegrooms also made gifts to the girl and her family, but the custom of a dowry never appears to have been adopted in Israel. On marriage the girl left her family and clan and she and her children became part of that of her husband.

We have no information about the age of marriage in New Testament times though we know that later the rabbis fixed the minimum age at twelve for girls, thirteen for boys. The parents were responsible for all decisions and arrangements. But the young people, at least in the biblical period, were very free: they looked after sheep (not only boys like David, but girls like Rachel, Genesis XXIX.6); gleaned in the fields, as did Dinah, Genesis XXXIV.1, and of course Ruth, (Ruth II.2), drew water (Gen. XXIV.13) and seem to have mixed freely with their menfolk. This of course sometimes led to trouble and this was strictly legislated for: the man who raped a virgin must marry her, must pay double the usual 'mohar' to her father and he might not divorce her. But the Israelite bride was no down-trodden slave, as the account of her in the passage quoted from Proverbs makes clear; she was truly mistress in her own household.

Betrothal

This was usual in New Testament times and seems to have lasted about a year. A girl who was unfaithful to her betrothed was subject to the same punishment as an unfaithful wife; but the betrothal could be terminated by either party on the payment of a fine.

Marriage Ceremonies

There was no religious sanction, marriage was purely a civil contract; the husband declared: 'She is my wife and I am her husband from this day for ever;' it is not recorded that the wife said anything. The chief ceremony was the entrance of the bride into the groom's house, accompanied by her friends:

> Where they lifted up their eyes, and looked. and, behold there was much ado and carriage: and the bridegroom came forth, and his friends and brethren, to meet them with four drums, and five instruments of music, and many weapons.
>
> (1 Maccabees IX.39)

and this procession is familiar to new Testament readers in the parable of the wise and foolish virgins, attending the bride, who went forth to meet the bridegroom's much-delayed procession to welcome the bride. (Matthew XXV.1ff) The bride was richly dressed and bejewelled:

17

> He hath covered me with the robe of righteousness, as a bridegroom decketh himself with a garland, and as a bride adorneth herself with her jewels.
>
> (Isiah LXI.10)

and she wore a veil which she removed only in the bridal chamber. (Thus was Laban enabled to cheat Jacob by substituting Leah for Rachel, Genesis XXIX.23.) A great feast followed in the bridegroom's house; the feast might last seven days or more. Jesus' first miracle is set by John at a marriage feast at Cana of Galilee; this feast was probably a small one in this small country village of poor people, and the wine ran out.

Divorce

The husband could divorce his wife:

> When a man taketh a wife, and marrieth her, then it shall be, if she find no favour in his eyes, because he found some unseemly thing in her, that he shall write her a bill of divorcement, and give into her hand, and send her out of his house.
>
> (Deuteronomy XXIV.1)

This bill of divorcement enabled the divorced woman to remarry, and if she had remarried the first husband was prohibited from marrying her again even if the second husband died. The provision of the bill of divorcement was to protect the wife but divorce was always frowned upon by the Jews, and still is today.

> Rejoice in the wife of thy youth.
>
> (Proverbs V.18)

> Live joyfully with the wife whom thou lovest all the days of the life of thy vanity, which he has given thee under the sun.
>
> (Ecclesiastes IX.9)

Malachi says that marriage makes two one and that a husband must keep the oath sworn to his partner for Yahweh hates divorce:

> For I hate putting away, saith the LORD God of Israel.
>
> (Malachi II.16)

The Rabbis Hillel and Shammai disputed about what constituted the 'unseemly thing' for which a man might divorce his wife: the latter limited the fault to unchastity, whereas the former said anything which displeased her husband, for instance a burned meal, constituted grounds for divorce. But there can be no doubt that the majority of rabbinic thinking was in accord with Jesus' teaching:

> There came unto him Pharisees, and asked him, Is it lawful for a man to put away his wife?...
>
> And he answered and said unto them, What did Moses command you?
>
> And they said, Moses suffered to write a bill of divorcement, and to put her away.
>
> But Jesus said unto them, For your hardness of heart he wrote you this commandment.
>
> But from the beginning of the creation, Male and female made he them.
>
> For this cause shall a man leave his father and mother, and shall cleave to his wife;
>
> And the twain shall be one flesh: so that they are no more twain, but one flesh.
>
> What therefore God has joined together, let not man put asunder.
>
> (Mark. X.2 to 9)

The argument is not that men do not exist and did not always exist who are hard of heart, but the ideal is not this; the ideal Jesus taught us is that of the prophets, of Israel's Wisdom teachers and of the Rabbis:

> When his wife dies a man's world is darkened, his step is slow, his mind is heavy; she dies in him, he in her.
>
> A man must not make a woman weep, for God counts her tears.

Though the Talmud warns against a foolish wife: 'A domineering wife makes life not worth living,' it does not counsel divorce. And the rabbis taught that man and wife, if they be deserving, have the Shekinah (God's presence) between them. We could not hope to find a higher ideal than that.

19

THE POSITION OF WOMEN

The woman's position was in the home, where she was supreme. It is noticeable that, from the earliest recension we have of the decalogue children are bidden to honour their 'father and mother', never the father alone. She was never a slave: a man could sell his slaves or even his daughters, but never his wife. As we have said, he could divorce her (she could never divorce him under Israelite law, although by Roman law she could) but by the bill of divorcement she regained her freedom.

In ancient Israel, all the hard work of the home fell on her; she looked after the flocks, worked in the fields, cooked the food, did the spinning. Sometimes even she took part in public affairs: Deborah 'judged Israel', Athalia reigned over Judah (Judges IV.5 and 2 Kings XI), Huldah was a prophetess, consulted by the king and his ministers (2 Kings XXII.14ff), Judith and Esther saved the nation. So 'career women' (and Huldah at least was married) existed even then. In the New Testament we are told that Philip the evangelist had four daughters, virgins, who prophesied (Acts XXI.9).

But her special and supreme sphere was and is in the home, where she has and has always had a unique dignity; in public worship her role is mainly passive, but she has her part to play at the Passover Seder and at the welcoming-in, in the home, of the Sabbath, where all the preparation is hers and hers the privilege of lighting the sabbath candles:

> The King's daughter within the palace is all glorious.
> (Psalm XLV.13)

Women, like slaves, are not bound by the affirmative precepts of the law; but this is no denigration of the woman, it is because a woman's domestic duties frequently make such observance impossible for her. Because Israel was a patriarchial society, widows and girls did not inherit, unless there were no sons, and then the heiress had to marry within her own tribe. Yet a Jewish child inherits his or her right to be a Jew from his mother; only the son of a Jewish mother is considered a Jew by the congregation, the son of a Gentile mother would not be accepted; doubtless this added to the mother's importance and respect for her within the family increased with the birth of the first child, especially if this child be a son; her husband

20

became more attached and his children owed her love and reverence. The law condemns offences against a mother equally with those against a father;

> And he that curseth his father, or his mother, shall surely be put to death.
>
> (Exodus XXI.17)

> If a man have a stubborn and rebellious son, which will not obey the voice of his father, or the voice of his mother, and though they chasten him will not hearken unto them:
>
> Then shall his father and his mother lay hold on him, and bring him out to the elders of the city...
>
> And they shall say...This our son is stubborn and rebellious, he will not obey our voice...
>
> (Deuteronomy XXI.18 to 20)

The disciplinary action taken in this case seems to be the mutual responsibility of both parents and to refer equally to disobedience to commands from either.

The Wisdom books insist on respect for one's mother:

> He that spoileth his father, and chaseth away his mother, is a son that causeth shame and bringeth reproach.
>
> (Proverbs XIX.26)

> Hearken unto thy father that begat thee, and despise not thy mother when she is old.
>
> (Proverbs XXIII.22)

> The LORD has given the father honour over the children, and hath confirmed the authority of the mother over the sons...
>
> He that honoreth his mother is as one that layeth up treasure...
>
> (Ecclesiasticus III.2ff)

> He that is obedient unto the LORD shall be a comfort to his mother...
>
> Honour thy father and mother...that a blessing may come upon thee from them...
>
> He that angereth his mother is cursed of God.
>
> (Ecclesiasticus III.6 ff)

21

A widow, especially one with children, might be in a piteous position, if she were not young enough to remarry, and the prophets are continually calling the attention of the pious to their plight; but God himself cares for them:

> God himself is their protector. (Psalm CXLVI.9)

The great respect accorded to the Jewish wife and mother was also marked among the early Christians. Indeed, women seem to have mixed more freely among Jesus' disciples than was customary among Jews at the time:

> And it came to pass soon afterwards that he went about through cities and villages, preaching and bringing the good tidings of the Kingdom of God and with him the twelve. And certain women that had been healed of evil spirits and infirmities, Mary that was Magdalene, from whom seven devils had gone out, and Joanna, the wife of Chuza, Herod's steward, and Suzanna, and many others, which ministered to them of their substance.
> (Luke VIII.1 to 3)

John says Jesus' disciples were 'astonished to find him talking with a woman' at the well (John VIII.5ff).

Mark tells us that at Jesus' death,

> There were also women beholding from afar; among whom were both Mary Magdalene and Mary the mother of James the Less and of Jose and Salome, who when he was in Galilee followed him; and many other women which came with him into Jerusalem.
> (Mark XV.40,41)

Women were the first witnesses of his resurrection and they were with the apostles between the Ascension and Pentecost:

> Those all with one accord continued steadfastly in prayer, with the women, and Mary the mother of Jesus and with his brethren.
> (Acts I.14)

The presence of women in the background helping can be seen all through the book of Acts. Women participated widely in Paul's ministry, as we can see from references in his epistles, and we know from the younger Pliny, writing to the Emperor Trajan about 200 A.D., that there were women deacons in the Christian churches in that region.

CHILDREN

Many children, like a good wife were much to be prized:

> Thy wife shall be like a fruitful vine, in the innermost parts of thine house: thy children like olive plants round about thy table.
> (Psalm CXXVIII.3)

> Lo, children are an heritage of the LORD: and the fruit of the womb is his reward.

> As arrows in the hand of a mighty man, so are the children of youth.

> Happy the man that hath his quiver full of them: they shall not be ashamed, when they speak with their enemies in the gate.
> (Psalm CXXVII.3ff)

The eldest son took precedence over his brothers even during his father's life-time:

> And they sat before him, the firstborn according to his birthright, and the youngest according to his youth...
> (Genesis XLIII.33)

and on his father's death he received a double share of the inheritance, became head of the family and, as we have seen, his inheritance was protected by law against favouritism by his father for one of his other sons. But he could lose this right, as Reuben did (Genesis XXXV.22 and XLIX.3ff) or he could relinquish it as Esau did (Genesis XXV.29ff) Also there were many exceptions which, the rabbis tell us, only show that God's choice is free. The firstborn belonged to God and must be redeemed: bought back. We see Mary and Joseph taking Jesus, their firstborn, to the temple to redeem him (Luke II.22ff). The ceremony of the redemption of the firstborn is still performed in Jewish synagogues today. In ancient Israel, the child seems to have been given a name immediately, but by New Testament times this was postponed until circumcision, on the eighth day. To name a person is to have power over him (hence, in reverence the Jews will not pronounce the Name of Yahweh) it also reveals his character and destiny. So, both John and Jesus receive their names from the angel who announces their birth.

Circumcision

It was the father's duty to ensure that his son was circumcised on the eighth day: this was done by the father at home. We have accounts of the circumcision of both John the Baptist (Luke I.59ff) and of Jesus (Luke II.21) The custom seems to have been practised by the patriarchs and Josephus says it was maintained in Egypt, certainly the Egyptians themselves were often circumcised, but it was forgotten in the desert and had to be resumed on entry into the Holy Land (Joshua V.3ff). It seems to have been common among Semitic peoples, but for Israel it had a special significance; it was the sign of incorporation into the community of Israel and the covenant. During the exile in Babylon it bacame the distinctive mark of the man who belonged to Israel and to Yahweh. According to Josephus, the Israelites were the only inhabitants of Palestine who practised it; the others must have abandoned it, for the biblical Canaanites were certainly circumcised, and it is held up as the shame of the Philistines that they were not. By New Testament times it had become the mark par excellence of the loyal Jew; the Greeks scorned the practice and, under Antiochus Epiphanes, Jews were put to death for circumcising their children. In John VII.22 we learn that the rite of circumcision took precedence even over the Sabbath. Full proselytes had to be circumcised before they could become Jews, and the practice was of course the matter of most bitter dispute in the early Christian Church; we have only to read the Acts of the Apostles, or many of Paul's epistles to meet the problem at every turn.

Bar Mitzvah

A Jewish boy becomes *bar mitzvah* (son of the covenant) at thirteen, and from that age he takes on full responsibility for the observance of the Law. The modern ceremony did not exist in New Testament times, but Jesus' parents took him up to the Temple, presumably for the first time and presumably to attend one of the pilgrim feasts, when he was twelve: i.e. when he was coming of age.

Education

During a child's early years the mother would inculcate in her children the first elements of training, including moral training, but as a boy grew older his father took over: girls remained with their mothers. We have seen that it was the father's duty to instruct his son in religion and also in a trade. Writing was in use from an early date; Deuteronomy VI.9 presumes that at least every head of a house could write; but most teaching was done by word of mouth. The teacher told the story and asked questions, the pupil repeated it and asked and answered questions; the same method was followed by the rabbis and is seen throughout Jesus' teaching in the New Testament.

Priests were guardians and teachers of the Law, and some instruction was probably given at places of worship: we have already instanced Jesus' appearance among the teachers in the Temple, 'both hearing them and asking them questions.'

After the exile there was probably at least a school for scribes where civil servants were trained, but formal schools were not common until fairly late: the first to be mentioned is in the Hebrew text of Sirach LI.23. Jewish tradition says that in A.D. 63 the High Priest Joshua ben Gimla decreed that every town and village should have a school and that all children should attend from the age of six or seven; but some scholars date the introduction of village schools from the time of John Hyrcanus, c.130 B.C. All we can say for certain is that the village school was coming into general existence in New Testament times.

These schools were for boys; girls remained with their mothers who taught them the duties of wives and housekeepers, and no doubt piety too.

DEATH AND FUNERAL RITES

The distinction between soul and body is not Hebrew: man was a *nephesh*, either living or dead; so long at least as his bones existed so did his soul in Sheol; so it was important that his corpse should have honourable burial. The corpse was buried fully clothed, not in a coffin but carried on a bier:

> And when he drew near to the gates of the city, behold there was carried out one that was dead, the only son of his mother, and she a widow...
>
> And when the Lord saw her, he had compassion on her, and said unto her, Weep not.
>
> And he came nigh and touched the bier: and the bearers stood still. And he said, Young man, I say unto thee, Arise.
>
> And he that was dead sat up, and began to speak...
>
> (Luke VII.12ff)

Such custom too is fully attested in the account of the raising of Lazarus (John XI.38ff) and in the accounts of Jesus' own burial and resurrection in all four Gospels: (Matthew XXVII.57ff and XXVIII 1 to 10: Mark XV.42ff and XVI 1 to 8; Luke XXIII.50ff and XXIV.1 to 12; John XIX.38ff and XX.1 to 18.)

From at least 100 B.C. to A.D. 100 the bodies were laid in tombs on ledges or in coffers of soft limestone, by those who could afford such burial, hence the importance for the Gospel writers of Joseph of Arimathea:

> And when even was come, there came a rich man from Arimathea, named Joseph...
>
> And Joseph took the body, and wrapped it in a clean cloth,
>
> And laid it in his own new tomb, which he had hewn out of the rock: and he rolled a great stone to the door of the tomb, and departed.
>
> (Matthew XXVII.57)

In the Kedron Valley there was the 'tomb of the sons of the people': a common trench where the poor were simply laid in the ground.

4. Social Justice

A concern for justice has always been part of the Hebrew religion, and justice spread out from the family to cover all: especially the widow and orphan and 'the stranger within thy gate'. Concern for the foreigner was every bit as alive among the prophets of the eighth century B.C. as concern for ethnic minorities is to us in the twentieth century A.D. Of the peoples of the ancient Middle East it is in Israel alone that slavery, although necessarily accepted as an institution, is challenged and the rights of the slave upheld, and that the power and greed of the wealthy are forcibly attacked. Moreover, in the Israelite law codes, there is a constant adaptation of laws about social justice to meet economic crises; for both law-maker and prophet there was no law or institution that was unalterable: everything could and should be developed to meet the new demands of the poor and defenceless.

In the surrounding countries there was one law for the aristocracy, another for the people, another for the slaves, and of course the king was above the law. It was not so in Israel: the law applied, at any rate in theory, to the king, to the priests and elders, to the people and to the slave and the stranger. David knew this when he lusted after the wife of one of his soldiers, and his condemnation by Israel's God called forth from the prophet Nathan one of the tenderest parables in the Bible (II Samuel XII.12ff), but when David had himself pronounced the condemnation of the rich man in the story, the prophet pronounced the damning words: 'thou art the man.'

Ahab of Israel knew it, when he sulked because he could not persuade Naboth to sell him the piece of land he coveted. But his wife, Jezebel, daughter of the priest-king of Tyre, had no patience with such scruples: kings were not thwarted by the whims of their subjects in her experience. So she swiftly arranged for a false accusation of treason to be brought against Naboth and for him to be found guilty and executed by the cowardly elders of Jezreel; then his patrimony, including the land Ahab wanted, reverted to the

27

king, and he went forth to possess it. But Yahweh's vengeance was swift and terrible:

> And the word of the LORD came to Elijah the Tishbite, saying: Arise, go down to meet Ahab of Israel...behold he is in the vineyard of Naboth, whither he is gone down to take possession of it.
>
> And thou shalt speak unto him, saying, Thus saith the LORD, in the place where the dogs licked the blood of Naboth shall the dogs lick thy blood, even thine...
>
> Behold thou hast sold thyself to do evil in the sight of the LORD.
>
> Behold I will bring evil upon thee, and will utterly sweep thee away, and will cut off from Ahab every man child...
>
> And of Jezebel also spake the LORD, saying, the dogs shall eat Jezebel by the rampart of Jezreel.
>
> (I Kings XXI.1ff)

Israel's God, unlike the pagan gods, always had a special care for the needy, the orphan, the widow and the stranger: 'Ye shall be holy, for I the LORD thy God am holy.' (Leviticus XIX.2). And the same book lays down instructions for the poor to be considered when the harvest is reaped:

> And when ye reap the harvest of your land, thou shalt not wholly reap the corners of thy field, neither shalt thou gather the gleanings of thy harvest.
>
> And thou shalt not glean thy vineyard, neither shalt thou gather the fallen fruit of thy vineyard: thou shalt leave them for the poor and for the stranger; I am the LORD your God.
>
> (Leviticus XIX.9 to 10)

and further:

> Thou shalt not oppress thy neighbour nor rob him; the wages of an hired servant shall not abide with thee all night until the morning.
>
> Thou shalt not curse the deaf, nor put a stumbling block before the blind, but thou shalt fear thy God: I am the LORD.
>
> (Leviticus XIX.13ff)
>
> Ye shall do no unrighteousness in judgment: thou shalt not respect (i.e. discriminate against) the person of the poor, nor honour the person of the mighty, but in righteousness thou shalt judge thy neighbour

(ibid. v.15)

And if a stranger sojourn in thy land, ye shall not do him wrong.

The stranger that sojourneth with you shall be to you as the home-born among you, and thou shalt love him as thyself; for ye were strangers in the land of Egypt: I am the LORD your God.

(ibid. vv. 32 to 34)

Every seventh year was a sabbatical year when the ground must be allowed to remain fallow and all might help themselves freely to its produce. Exodus XXIII verses 10 and 11 make it clear that this is for the benefit of the poor (as well as for the good of the land):

And six years thou shalt sow thy land, and shalt gather the increase thereof: But the seventh year thou shalt let it rest and lie fallow; that the poor of thy people may eat. In like manner thou shall deal with thy vineyard, and with thy oliveyard.

Moreover the forty-ninth year (7 times 7), or some think the fiftieth year, was especially holy: it was the year of jubilee, when there was general freedom throughout the land; every man returned to his home or clan and all land, which had been sold in distress, reverted to its original owner or his heirs; thus preventing the rich from 'joining field to field.'

Unfortunately, as the kingdoms of Israel and Judah became worldly and wealthy, these ideals were not always lived up to; but the Hebrews never accepted this back-sliding or became reconciled to it and the castigation thundered out by her prophets equals anything the twentieth century can do. For Israel, justice to the poor, the weak, the deprived was always linked to the right attitude to her holy and just God:

Learn to do well; seek judgment, relieve the oppressed, judge the fatherless, plead for the widow.

(Isaiah I.17)

The LORD will enter into judgment with the elders of the people, and the princes thereof; it is ye that have eaten up the vineyard, the spoil of the poor is in your houses:

What mean ye that ye crush my people, and grind the face of the poor? saith the LORD, the LORD of Hosts.

(Isaiah III.14,15)

Woe to them that join house to house, that lay field to field, till there be no room.

(Isaiah V.8)

And they covet fields, and take them; and houses and take them away.

(Micah II.2)

Therefore, thus saith the LORD: Behold against this family do I devise an evil, from which ye shall not remove your necks...

(Micah II.2,3)

Thus saith the LORD: For three transgression of Israel, yea for four, I will not turn away the punishment thereof; because they have sold the righteous for silver, and the needy for a pair of shoes:

That pant after the dust of the earth on the head of the poor, and turn aside the way of the meek.

(Amos II.6,7)

Hear this word, ye kine (i.e. women) of Bashan, that are on the mountains of Samaria, which oppress the poor, which crush the needy, which say unto their lords: Bring and let me drink.

The LORD has sworn by his holiness that, lo, the days shall come upon you, that they shall take you away with hooks, and your residue with fish hooks.

(Amos IV.1,2)

Seek the LORD and ye shall live, lest he break out like a fire in the house of Joseph, and it devour and there be none to quench it...

Ye who turn judgment to wormwood, and cast down righteousness to the earth...

Forasmuch therefore as ye trample upon the poor, and take exactions from him of wheat; ye have built houses of hewn stone, but ye shall not dwell in them; ye have planted pleasant vineyards, but ye shall not drink the wine thereof.

For I know how manifold are your transgressons and how mighty your sins; ye that afflict the just, that take a bribe, and that turn aside the needy in the gate...

Therefore thus saith the LORD, the God of Hosts, the LORD: Wailing shall be in all the broad ways, and they shall say in all the streets: Alas! Alas! and they shall call the husbandman to mourning, and such as are skilful of lamentation to wailing...for I will pass through the midst of thee, saith the LORD.

(Amos V.11 to 17)

For I desire mercy, and not sacrifice; and the knowledge of God
more than burnt offerings.

(Hosea VI.6)

This last is quoted by Jesus (Matthew XII.7) The last of the
Hebrew prophets summed up this teaching:

Have we not one father? Hath not one God created us? Why do
we deal treacherously every man against his brother; prophaning
the covenant of our fathers?

(Malachi II.10)

This social injustice, as well as her unfaithfulness to her God
in going after pagan idols, was always seen as the cause of the
exile from the Holy Land of the kingdoms of both Israel and
Judah: an exile from which only a remnant returned. This remnant had learned its lesson and remained henceforce unswervingly
faithful to the One God. Although human nature is always liable
to swerve from the ideal, her teachers never failed to insist upon
the requirement of charity to the poor, the needy, the orphan, the
widow, the fatherless and the stranger. The rabbis have always
taught that this is one of the chief ways a man may atone for his
sins and become reconciled with his God, who is a God of mercy,
justice and compassion. This conviction is as alive today as it was
among the ancient Hebrews and the great prophets who thundered
out Yahweh's call to care for his poor: the expression 'the poor of
Yahweh' is common in the Bible.

He hath shown thee, O man, what is good; and what doth the
LORD require of thee, but to do justly, and to love mercy, and
to walk humbly with thy God.

(Micah VI.8)

Perhaps the world has never been so much in need of this teaching,
and certainly it has never been more conscious of its need. May we
go forward, with this ideal which we have inherited from and share
with our Jewish brethren and, together with them, advance towards
its increasing realization.

5. The Hebrew Calendar

The basic unit, as everywhere, was the solar day: morning, evening and night. Creation seems to have begun in the morning and gone on till nightfall, after which there was 'evening and there was morning, one day': i.e. evening, after the day in which God created light, then night and when light came again one day was over.

> In the morning thou shalt say, 'Would God it were even! and at even thou shalt say, Would God it were morning...'
>
> (Deuteronomy XXVIII.67)

But in the later books the expression 'day and night' became reversed; e.g. Judith begins her prayer at the time of the evening offering (Judith IX.1). Psalm LV speaks of prayer 'at evening, at morning and at noon' and this was certainly the reckoning used in New Testament times, just it is among Jews to the present day. We might instance Jesus' healings at Caphernaum. He had healed Simon's wife's mother in the morning, after they had returned home from the synagogue and the news had spread through the village during the Sabbath day's rest; then,

> At even, when the sun did set, they brought unto him all that were sick, and them that were possessed of devils...
>
> and he healed many that were sick of divers diseases, and cast out many devils;
>
> And in the morning, a great while before day, he rose up, and departed into a desert place and there prayed.
>
> (Mark. I.32ff)

The month, however, was reckoned by the moon, a new month being reckoned from when the new moon appeared. As a full lunar month takes twenty-nine days, twelve hours and a fraction, the months were reckoned as having twenty-nine days and thirty days alternately. Twelve lunar months resulted in three hundred and fifty-four days, eight hours and a fraction; but the year based on the sun had three-hundred and sixty-five days; this difficulty was overcome by introducing, from time to time, an intercalary, extra month of Adar; this is still the Jewish practice. At first the months were given Canaanite names, connected with the seasons, but later, by New Testament times, the Babylonian names had been accepted:

I Nisan	(March/April)
II Iyar	(April/May)
III Sivan	(May/June)
IV Tammuz	(June/July)
V Av	(July/August)
VI Elul	(August September)
VII Tishri	(September/October)
VIII Cheshvan	(October/November)
IX Kislev	(November/December)
X Tevet	(December/January)
XI Shevat	(January/February)
XII Adar	(February/March)

Josephus uses this system.

The only period of less than a month for which we have good evidence is the week, of seven days; its origin is obscure, but perhaps it derives from the sacred number of seven, for completion: i.e. three is the number of the heavens and four the number of the earth, since it has four corners, so seven is completion, heaven and earth. It must be independent of the lunar month, which is not divisible into weeks, so the week came to be the centre of a cycle of its own, marked by a day of repose on the seventh day: the Sabbath, peculiar to Israel. The only feast which continued to fall on the same day each year was the Sabbath. In the Book of Jubilees, by contrast, the year is governed by the week, a year having fifty-two weeks, three hundred and sixty-four days, divided into quarters of thirteen weeks, i.e. ninety-one days. Seven years are a week of years, as in Daniel, and seven weeks of years form a jubilee. This reckoning is also found in Enoch and in the Qumram literature. It had the effect of ensuring that feasts always fell on the same day each year. This reckoning may have been known in New

The Christian Year 1989

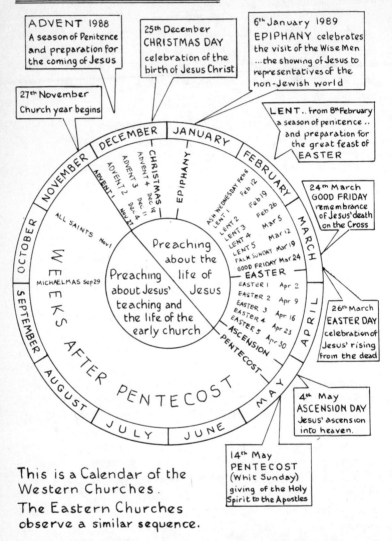

ADVENT 1988
A season of Penitence and preparation for the coming of Jesus

25th December
CHRISTMAS DAY
celebration of the birth of Jesus Christ

6th January 1989
EPIPHANY celebrates the visit of the Wise Men ...the showing of Jesus to representatives of the non-Jewish world

27th November
Church year begins

LENT.. from 8th February a season of penitence .. and preparation for the great feast of **EASTER**

24th March
GOOD FRIDAY
remembrance of Jesus' death on the Cross

26th March
EASTER DAY
celebration of Jesus' rising from the dead

4th May
ASCENSION DAY
Jesus' ascension into heaven.

14th May
PENTECOST
(Whit Sunday)
giving of the Holy Spirit to the Apostles

Within the wheel:

NOVEMBER — DECEMBER — JANUARY — FEBRUARY — MARCH — APRIL — MAY — JUNE — JULY — AUGUST — SEPTEMBER — OCTOBER

ADVENT 1 Nov 27
ADVENT 2 Dec 4
ADVENT 3 Dec 11
ADVENT 4 Dec 18
CHRISTMAS
EPIPHANY
ASH WEDNESDAY Feb 8
LENT 1 Feb 12
LENT 2 Feb 19
LENT 3 Feb 26
LENT 4 Mar 5
LENT 5 Mar 12
PALM SUNDAY Mar 19
GOOD FRIDAY Mar 24
EASTER
EASTER 1 Apr 2
EASTER 2 Apr 9
EASTER 3 Apr 16
EASTER 4 Apr 23
EASTER 5 Apr 30
ASCENSION
PENTECOST

ALL SAINTS Nov 1
MICHAELMAS Sep 29

WEEKS AFTER PENTECOST

Preaching about the life of Jesus
Preaching about Jesus' teaching and the life of the early church

This is a Calendar of the Western Churches.
The Eastern Churches observe a similar sequence.

Dates of movable Feasts and Fasts in each year can be found in Whitacker's Almanack.

Guy Wickenden
14 . VI . 88

34

The Jewish Year 5749

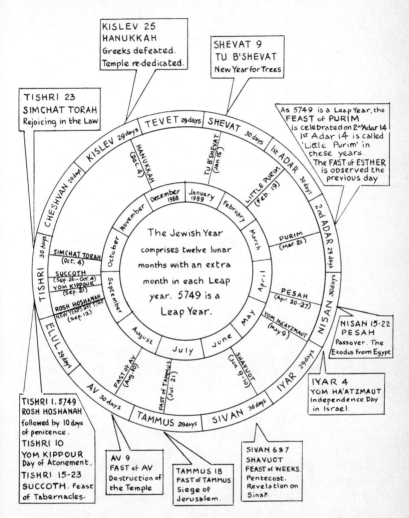

KISLEV 25
HANUKKAH
Greeks defeated.
Temple re-dedicated.

SHEVAT 9
TU B'SHEVAT
New Year for Trees

TISHRI 23
SIMCHAT TORAH
Rejoicing in the Law

As 5749 is a Leap Year, the
FEAST of PURIM
is celebrated on 2nd Adar 14
1st Adar 14 is called
'Little Purim' in
these years.
The FAST of ESTHER
is observed the
previous day

NISAN 15-22
PESAH
Passover. The
Exodus from Egypt

IYAR 4
YOM HA'ATZMAUT
Independence Day
in Israel.

SIVAN 6 & 7
SHAVUOT
FEAST of WEEKS.
Pentecost.
Revelation on
Sinai.

TAMMUS 18
FAST of TAMMUS
Siege of
Jerusalem.

AV 9
FAST of AV
Destruction of
the Temple

TISHRI 1, 5749
ROSH HOSHANAH
followed by 10 days
of penitence.
TISHRI 10
YOM KIPPOUR
Day of Atonement.
TISHRI 15-23
SUCCOTH. Feast
of Tabernacles.

Inner ring (calendar wheel):

CHESHVAN 29days · KISLEV 29days · HANUKKAH (Dec. 4) · TEVET 29days · SHEVAT 30days · TU B'SHEVAT (Jan 15) · 1st ADAR 30days · LITTLE PURIM (Feb. 9) · 2nd ADAR 29days · PURIM (Mar. 21) · NISAN 30days · PESAH (Apr. 20-27) · YOM HA'ATZMAUT (May 9) · IYAR 29days · SHAVUOT (Jun. 9-10) · SIVAN 30days · TAMMUS 29days · FAST OF TAMMUS (Jul. 21) · FAST OF AV (Aug. 10) · AV 30days · ELUL 29days · TISHRI 30 days · SIMCHAT TORAH (Oct. 4) · SUCCOTH (Sep. 26 - Oct. 4) · YOM KIPPOUR (Sep. 21) · ROSH HOSHANAH NEW YEARS DAY 5749 (Sep. 12)

Civil months ring:

December 1988 · November · October · September · August · July · June · May · April · March · February · January 1989

The Jewish Year
comprises twelve lunar
months with an extra
month in each Leap
year. 5749 is a
Leap Year.

This calendar shows the current Jewish Year beginning in the month
of Tishri; the book uses the year beginning in the month of Nisan.

The dates of Jewish Feasts, Fasts and their civilian equivalents can be found in the Jewish Year Book

35

Testament times, but it cannot have been maintained for very long since there is nowhere any mention of adjustments to accommodate a year of three-hundred and sixty-five and a quarter days.

The days do not seem to have had distinctive names in Israel, though Friday was sometimes called the eve of the Sabbath or the Preparation and Sunday the day following the Sabbath; but otherwise they were simply referred to by numbers, Monday being the first day and the Sabbath the seventh day of the week.

New Year

The two oldest liturgical calendars (Exodus XXIII.14 to 17, and Exodus XXXIV.18 to 23) mark three great annual feasts: Unleavened Bread, Harvest and Ingathering, the last of which fell 'at the going out' of the year: i.e. at its beginning, therefore the Jewish year began in the autumn, as it does today.

But other texts differ. When Jeremiah's prophecies were read to Jehoiakim he was sitting in his winter house with a brazier beside him in which he burned the strips of parchment as he read, and it was 'the ninth month' so evidently the year must have begun in the spring. According to 2 Kings XXV.8 ff and Jeremiah LII.12 the temple was destroyed by Nebuchadnezzar in the fifth month, and both Josephus and Jewish tradition say it was at the same time of the year that the second temple was destroyed by Titus, and we know that this was in August. So it would seem that by the time of Josiah, the Babylonian year beginning in the spring had been adopted. It would seem probable that Israel observed the autumn calendar while independent and that the Babylonian calendar was imposed, at least for official use in the Assyrian provinces in the eighth century and in Judah after Josiah's death, under his son Jehoiakim.

But the year beginning in the autumn does not seem to have died out entirely. Josephus explains the two calendars by saying that the Nisan calendar was the ecclesiastical calendar and the Tishri one the civil (Antiquities I.3.3) The rabbis, puzzled by the different texts, since at the time their different dates were not distinguished, reckoned on four different dates for the beginning of the New Year: in Nisan, for the reigns of kings and for festivals, in Elul for the tithe on cattle, in Tishri the New Year for years and for Sabbaths and the jubilee year, and in Shevat for the tithe on trees.

In New Testament times the great feast of Rosh Hashanah was already being kept, on 1st Tishri, the seventh month in the Babylonian calendar; but how far this was observed as a New Year feast is disputed among scholars. Probably we shall not be far wrong if we follow Josephus' distinction and think of a liturgical year beginning in Nisan (the spring) and a civil year beginning in Tishri (the autumn).

The Sabbath

The origin of this day is not clear from the Bible. The account of the gathering of manna in Exodus XVI. 22 to 30 implies that Sabbath regulations were in force before the giving of the Law on Sinai; for whereas if the people gathered more than enough manna for one day at a time during the first five days what was left over went bad by the next day, on the sixth day they were instructed to gather enough for two days, since there would be none to gather on the Sabbath, and that left over for the seventh did not 'stink, neither was there any worm therein.'

The priestly account of the creation, in Genesis II, says it existed from the beginning:

> And on the seventh day God finished his work which he had made; and he rested on the seventh day...
>
> And God blessed the seventh day, and hallowed it: because that in it he rested from all his work which God had created and made.
> (Genesis II.2,3)

It is from the beginning intrinsically connected with Yahwism and in Israel it took on a significance it did not have before. It is found in all the different traditions in the Pentateuch and always on the seventh day, when man rests from his six days of work. Picking a rest day was of course worldwide, but in Israel it was distinctive because this day was holy, related to God and his Covenant; for six days He was busy creating the world and all its furnishings, but on the seventh He rested and had leisure to make his Covenant with man. Two different motives for man to observe

37

this day are given. There is the social aspect of the Sabbath and also it is connected with the history of salvation; God's delivery of his people from Egypt and the desert and his bringing them in to rest of the Promised Land (Dueteronomy V. 14 and 15 and Exodus XXIII.12):

> But the seventh day is the sabbath of the LORD thy God: in it thou shalt not do any work, thou, nor thy son, nor thy daughter, nor thy manservant, nor thy maidservant, nor thine ox, nor thine ass, nor any of thy cattle, nor thy stranger that is within thy gates; that thy manservant and thy maidservant may rest as well as thou.

> And thou shalt remember that thou wast a servant in the land of Egypt, and the LORD thy God brought thee out thence by a mighty hand and by a stretched out arm; therefore the LORD thy God commanded thee to keep the sabbath day.
>
> (Deuteronomy V.14,15)

Since it was a sign of the Covenant, to observe it was a guarantee of salvation:

> If thou turn away thy foot from the sabbath, from doing thy pleasure on my holy day; and call the sabbath a delight, and the holy of the LORD honourable, and shalt honour it, not doing thine own own ways, nor finding thine own pleasure,...

> Then shalt thou delight thyself in the LORD...
>
> (Isaiah LVIII.13,14)

But this text is post-exilic and we can see the sabbath regulations tightening up; it is still a delight (the Jewish sabbath never fell into the straight-jacket of the Puritan 'Sabbath,' kept on Sunday), but after the exile what had been a pleasant rest day, to visit friends, or a man of God, or the local sanctuary became more and more a day on which things must be refrained from. Jesus did not attack the observance of the sabbath as such, but the forcing of taboos on what was meant to be a joyous day: 'The sabbath was made for man, and not man for the sabbath.' (Mark II.27) is echoed in the second century A.D. rabbinic gloss of Exodus XXXI.14: 'The sabbath was given to you; you were not given to the sabbath.'

The early Christians observed the Sabbath and followed it by the observance of their own particular liturgy, and this, as well as the fact that Jesus rose on the first day of the week, and so on that day began Christianity, as the *Didach* (an early second-century Christian work) points out, may have been contributary to the adoption of Sunday, the first day of the week, by the Christian Church. In the story of Eutychus in Acts we see this happening:

> And upon the first day of the week, when we were gathered together to break bread, Paul discoursed with them, intending to depart on the morrow; and prolonged his speech until midnight.
>
> (Acts XX.7)

This presumably was the night after the Sabbath, i.e. the Saturday night running on into Sunday morning.

The two days are still observed by Jews and Christians respectively, and they have much in common: both are days of rest from hard labour and a time to give special attention to religious duties, as well as a time to enjoy oneself and to rejoice in family reunions. Admittedly this has become much less so in modern society, both Jewish and Christian, but it may be as well for us both to remind ourselves of the origin of this day of rest and its connection from earliest times with God's goodness to his people.

6. Worship

THE TEMPLE

The temple worship was always sacrificial, as was the worship of all Israel's neighbours; but sacrifice was always accompanied by prayer and by liturgical actions such as singing (the books of psalms were the hymnbook of the temple) by processions, trumpet blowings and palm waving on festivals, and by reading from the Torah and instruction therein. Sacrifices were not only of animals, they also included the offering of incense and of cereals and libations of wine.

In ancient Israel, sacrifice was offered at the local shrines and was usually a joyous occasion, when a man came with his family and friends to offer a peace offering or a communion sacrifice. The blood was poured out to Yahweh, for it was believed that the life resided in the blood and life was sacred to God. The rest of the sacrifice, having been offered on the altar and a portion reserved for the officiating priest, was given to the worshipper to share with his family and friends in a festal meal in God's honour.

However, sacrificial worship at local shrines, being superficially very similar to that being offered by pagans, was in danger of becoming synchronistic, that is, adopting pagan customs. For this reason King Josiah in his great reform, shortly before the destruction of Jerusalem and the carrying off of her leading people to exile, forbade all sacrifice at local shrines: only in Jerusalem might sacrifice be offered. This meant that with the destruction of the Temple and Jerusalem itself in 587 B.C. there was no longer sacrifice in Israel or Judah. The exiles who returned from Babylon restored the temple and sacrificial worship, but with the destruction of Jerusalem and the temple by Titus in A.D. 70 sacrificial worship came to an end in Israel. This was extremely bitter to the people, so prophets and rabbis worked hard, as they had done among the

Babylonian exiles, to reassure them that sin can be taken away by good deeds and not only by sacrifice. They taught: 'God forgives him who forgives his neighbour.' The three means of atonement were prayer, almsgiving and repentance; there is confession of sin in both morning and evening prayer and they taught that even the wicked can reverse the judgment against them by repentance:

> The soul that sinneth it shall die...

> But if the wicked turn away from his sins...and keep all my statutes, and do that which is lawful and right, he shall surely live and shall not die.
>
> (Ezekiel XVIII.20,21)

Here the prophet is reassuring his fellow exiles that, although they can no longer expiate their sins by sacrifice, yet God will forgive the sinner if he repents and shows his repentence in good works. But some rabbis taught that, for some sins, forgiveness was impossible; especially for the man who caused others to sin. They were hard on heretics, apostates and unbelievers.

The early Christian fathers frequently taught that there was no forgiveness for apostasy and this seems to have been the view of the writer of the Epistle to the Hebrews:

> Those who were once enlightened...and then fall away: it is impossible to renew them unto repentence.
>
> (Hebrews VI.6)

But we have no such teaching from Jesus: the only sin he says cannot be forgiven is a sin 'against the holy spirit' and this is said in connection with those who are saying that he is acting in league with the devil, not by the hand of God: i.e. their sin is the refusal to see, to acknowledge that Jesus' action comes from God and therefore they have cut themselves off from all access to grace:

> Verily I say unto you, all their sins shall be forgiven unto the sons of men, and their blasphemies wherewith soever they have blasphemed:

> But whosoever shall blaspheme against the holy spirit hath never forgiveness: but is guilty of an eternal sin.
>
> (Mark III.28,29)

41

However, to return to the destruction of the temple, the rabbis had a hard time trying to convince the people that sacrifice was not necessary to forgiveness, and to this day the synagogue service contains long accounts of the sacrifices offered in the temple, so that the worshippers may unite themselves with their intentions. We know that Judaism was mocked by pagans for having no sacrifice, as, it seems, Christianity was too, since it is the aim of the writer of the Epistle to the Hebrews to show that Christianity does have a sacrifice, Jesus' sacrifice on the cross, which was the culmination of all the temporary sacrifices offered in the temple, so that no other sacrifice is any longer required.

The prophets did not condemn sacrifice (it was the accepted form of worship). What they did condemn was a sacrifice which was not accompanied by sincere worship of the heart:

> Sacrifice and offering thou hast no delight in; mine ears hast thou opened: burnt offering and sin offering hast thou not required.
>
> Then said I, Lo, I come;...
>
> I delight to do thy will, O my God, yea, thy law is within my heart.
> (Psalm XL.7ff)

> For thou delightest not in sacrifice, else would I give it: thou hast no pleasure in burnt offering. The sacrifices of God are a broken spirit: a broken and a contrite heart, O God, thou wilt not despise.
> (Psalm LI.16,17)

Jesus' parents, when they brought him to redeem him, their firstborn, in the temple (Luke II.24) brought with them a sacrifice 'according to that which is said in the law of the Lord.' Jesus and his disciples attended the temple sacrifices when they went up to the temple three times a year for the pilgrim feasts. But as time went on, it began to be understood, both in Judaism and Christianity that what God required was a spiritual sacrifice: obedience, a contrite heart, love and humility:

> I beseech you therefore, brethren, by the mercies of God, to present your bodies a living sacrifice, holy, acceptabe to God...
>
> be ye transformed...that ye may prove what is good and acceptable and perfect will of God.
> (Romans XII.1,2)

However, it is from the synagogue, rather that the temple, that Christianity derives its liturgy.

THE SYNAGOGUE

This was a place for prayer, reading the Law and instruction. Perhaps it originated in Babylon during the exile, or perhaps it was the result of Josiah's reform, when the local sanctuaries were destroyed. Our oldest evidence is from Josephus (Jewish Wars VIII.3.3.), who tells us that there was one at Antioch under Antiochus Ephiphanes. At any rate there is no question but that they were widespread throughout Palestine, including Jerusalem itself, and throughout the Diaspora in New Testament times. Jesus is constantly seen, in all four Gospels, attending the local synagogues where he taught and healed. The first Christians, we see; '..day by day, continuing steadfastly with one accord in the temple, and breaking bread at home...' (Acts. II.46).

We know, too, that Paul and Barnabas, on their missionary tours, always went first to the Jewish synagogue, if there was one in the city or village they came to, and preached to the Jews and proselytes who attended it; only when they were opposed and turned out did they go elsewhere; in this they enacted in miniature what was to be the pattern for the growing Christian Church. After A.D. 70, sacrifice, which as we have seen was central to the cult, was no longer possible, and prayer and the reading and study of the scriptures became of increasing importance; for this the synagogue was the place.

There were three synagogue services each day, evening, morning and mid-day; just as there had been sacrifices in the temple at these times.

The arrangement of the prayers in the synagogue are still familiar to us in the arrangement of our Christian services, which are obviously derived from there. They consist of praise and petition, more of the former than the latter as a rule, and of readings from the Torah, from the prophets, the writings, and the singing of the psalms, with instruction on the Torah and the Scriptures. Clearly the early Christians, forbidden to enter the synagogue, continued the synagogual practices in their own places of meeting, simply adding their own liturgy of the 'breaking of bread.'

The Jewish liturgy nowadays shows the growth of many centuries and it is sometimes very difficult or even impossible to tell what the original form was; but since it gave rise to the form of worship we know it seems well worth while to try to establish at least the minimum which we can be sure was known to Jesus and his disciples and to the early Church.

The earliest form of the Mishnah shows three daily services on ordinary days with the two main elements: prayer and the reading of the Scriptures. The Torah was always read on Sabbaths and on Mondays and Thursdays (market day in Palestine) and on feast days. In addition, on Sabbaths and feast days, a passage was read from the prophetic books. These readings were in Hebrew, but were followed immediately by a translation into the vernacular or by an explanation or exposition. If a distinguised guest was present he might be called upon to choose a passage from the prophets, read it and give an exposition; we see this custom in operation in Luke IV. 16 ff:

> And he came to Nazareth, where he had been brought up: and he entered, as his custom was, into the synagogue on the sabbath day, and stood up to read.
>
> And there was delivered unto him the book of the prophet Isaiah. And he opened the book, and found the place where it was written, The Spirit of the Lord is upon me, because he anointed me to preach good tidings to the poor: He hath sent me to proclaim release to the captives, and recovering of sight to the blind, to set at liberty them that are bruised,
>
> To proclaim the acceptable year of the Lord.
>
> And he closed the book and gave it back to the attendant, and sat down: and the eyes of all in the synagogue were fastened upon him.
>
> And he began to say unto them, Today hath this scripture been fulfilled in your ears.
>
> And all bare him witness, and wondered at the words of grace which proceeded out of his mouth.

Rabbi Gamaliel II of Jamnia, i.e. in the late New Testament period, was the great spiritual leader who ordered the texts and prayers which were to be used in the synagogues. He ordered the *Amidah* Prayer, called The Eighteen Benedictions, to be recited daily; the first three and the last three benedictions were fixed, the middle ones changing with the seasons, and it was he who added another, numbered the twelfth, against heretics, including Christians. The early Christians must have been familiar at least with the major part of this prayer, and an attempt will be made below to identify what appear to be the oldest parts. But prayers were still largely spontaneous and others were handed down orally, and there was a certain reluctance to write them down for fear that sectarians, heretics including Christians might write down prayers and insert into them their own ideas. And it was quite likely because of the Christian claim that God laid down *only* the ten commandments and no other laws that the reading of these daily in the synagogue, which seems to have been customary in the time of Jesus, was abandoned. Their reading used to be customary in Christian Churches at morning service; perhaps the church took over what the synagogue abandoned.

Of course every Israelite from the age of five was obliged to repeat the *Shema*: 'Hear O Israel, the Lord our God, the Lord is one Lord,' first thing every morning and before lying down every night, and at the hour of death. We may be quite sure that, if we had a firsthand account of the Crucifixion, Jesus' last words would have been these. So strongly was this the foundation of Israel's faith that it informed all the doctrinal arguments of Christian theologians throughout the first four centuries of Christianity, culminating in 325, at the Council of Nicea, with the first statement of the definitive creed: 'I believe in ONE God.' The Shema consisted of Deuteronomy VI.4 to which was added later Deuteronomy VI.5 and XI. 13 to 21 with Numbers XV 37 to 41:

> Hear, O Israel, the LORD our God is one LORD. And thou shalt love the LORD thy God with all thine heart, and with all thy soul, and with all thy might.

This much at least was current in New Testament times since it is quoted by Jesus in Mark XII. 29 and 30.

The *Shema* was publicly recited daily in the temple and synagogue and was preceded and followed by benedictions, two before and two (one in the morning) after it. These are known by their opening words: *Yotser* (Creator), *Ahabah* (love) *Emethwe-Yatzib* (true and constant) or *Geullah* (Redemption) from the concluding words, and *Hashkibenu* (Cause us to lie down).

Yotser has clearly been much lengthened in the course of time; scholars are divided about its exact wording but a probable approximation to its original wording may be:

> Blessed are Thou, O Lord our God, King of the universe, who formest light and createst darkness; who makest peace and createst all things; who givest light in mercy to the earth to those who live thereon, and in goodness renewest every day continually the work of creation. Be thou blessed, O Lord our God, for the excellence of the work of thy hands, and for the bright luminaries which thou hast made, let them glorify thee. Selah. Blessed art Thou, O Lord, who formest the lunimaries.

Ahabah is much shorter and has probably received few additions. In *Yotser* God is glorified as the giver of material light to the earth; in *Ahabah*, prayer is offered for spiritual light; it has been called one of the most beautiful prayers in the liturgies of the world:

> With great love Thou hast loved us, O Lord our God, with great and overflowing pity thou hast pitied us. O our Father, our King, for the sake of our fathers, who trusted in Thee, and to whom Thou didst teach the statutes of life, be generous unto us too and teach us. Enlighten our eyes in thy Law, and let our hearts cleave unto thy commandments, and unite our hearts to love and fear thy Name, that we may never be put to confusion. For Thou art a God that workest salvation, and Thou hast chosen us from every people and tongue, and hast brought us near unto thy great name, Selah, in faithfulness to give thanks unto Thee, and to proclaim thy Unity, in love. Blessed art Thou, O Lord, who choosest thy people Israel in love.

The text of *Guellah* may originally have been shorter, but most of the additions are agreed to be early:

True and constant, established and enduring, right and faithful, beloved and precious, desired and pleasing, awe- inspiring and mighty, well ordered and acceptable, good and lovely, is thy word unto us for ever and ever. It is true that the God of the Universe is our King, the Rock of Jacob, the Shield of Salvation to generation and generation He endureth, and his Name endureth. His throne is established and his kingdom and his faithfulness endure for ever. His words are living and enduring, faithful and desirable for ever and unto ages of ages, for our fathers and for us, and for our children and for our generations, and for the generations of the seed of thy servant Israel. It is true that Thou art He who art the Lord our God, and the God of our fathers, our King and the King of our fathers; our Maker and the Rock of our Salvation; our Liberator and our Deliverer for everlasting; that is thy Name; there is no God beside Thee.

Here follows a long passage which some consider as an addition although it seems to provide the basis of some early Christian prayers, which points to its being of pre-Christian date: but it is too long to include here. The prayer continues:

With a new song did the redeemed praise thy Name on the sea- shore; with one accord they gave thanks and acknowledged thy Kingship, and said, 'the Lord shall reign for evermore.' O Rock of Israel arise to the help of Israel, and deliver Judah and Israel according to thy promise. Our Redeemer, the Lord of Hosts is his Name, the Holy One of Israel. Blessed art Thou O Lord who hast redeemed Israel.

Hashkibene (Cause us to lie down) is added at evening service. Its antiquity is not as firmly established as that of the other three; but a second benediction said after the *Shema* in the evening service is mentioned in the Mishnah and presumably refers to this prayer.

Cause us to lie down, O Lord our God, in peace; and cause us to rise, O our King, to life. And spread over us the tabernacle of thy peace; and guide us by thy good counsel. Deliver us for thy Name's sake, and be a shield about us. Keep far from us every enemy: pestilence and sword, hunger and grief; drive away the evil one from before and behind us. Shelter us under the shadow of thy wings, for Thou O God art our Guardian and Deliverer; for Thou O God art a merciful King. Guard our going out and coming in, that it may be for life and peace, from henceforth and for ever. Blessed art Thou, O Lord, who guardest thy people Israel for ever.

It seems reasonable to assume that the *Shema* and its blessings formed the first part of our early Christian liturgy and that this was followed, as now, by more prayer and the reading and exposition of the scriptures. There were no prayer books but frequent repetition tended to fix the form of words, and varied circumstances would call forth special prayers, sometimes extemporare; little seems to have been written down before the fourth or fifth century, by which time the Christian Church had its own liturgy: but comparisons made by scholars show very close parallels. Praise and thanksgiving are the dominant note in Jewish prayers, actual petitions take a subordinate place, hence a prayer came to be called *Berakah* (a benediction) and each prayer ended with a doxology. They praise God's power and might in creation, his guardianship of his people, and his love in his delivery of them from Egypt and from all evil. A good example is the great prayer in Nehemiah IX; we are told here that the people:

> were assembled with fasting, and with sackcloth, and earth upon them.
>
> and the seed of Israel separated themselves from all strangers, and stood and confessed their sins...
>
> And they stood up in their place, and read in the book of the law of the LORD their God a fourth part of the day; and another fourth part they confessed, and worshipped the LORD their God...
>
> Then the Levites...said, Stand up and bless the LORD your God from everlasting to everlasting: and blessed be thy glorious name, which is exalted above all blessing and praise.
>
> (Nehemiah IX.1ff)

This is followed by a long historical retrospect (Judaism, like Christianity, has always been an historical religion) praising God for his goodness to his people: in the choice of Abram, in giving his people the Land of Canaan, in seeing their affliction and bringing them out of Egypt and through the desert, in the giving of the law at Sinai: then it remembers Israel's stubborn faithlessness, yet He forgave them and brought them into the land and it goes on to tell of Israel's continued unfaithfulness and God's continual love and forgiveness, even to the present time, and ends:

> And yet for all this we make a sure covenant, and write it; and our princes, our Levites, and our priests, seal unto it.
>
> (Nehemiah IX.38)

All the prayers have a corporate sense; they are in the first person plural and concern the whole community of Israel; and there was intercession on behalf of those outside as well. Darius (Ezra VI) requests that the people should:

> Offer sacrifices of sweet savour unto the God of heaven, and pray for the life of the king, and of his sons.
>
> (verse 10)

Josephus tells us (Antiquities XII.ii.6) that Eleazar the high priest, in writing to Ptolomy King of Egypt says:

> We immediately, therefore, offered sacrifices for thee and thy sister, with thy children and friends; and the multitude made prayers, that thy affairs may be to thy mind, and that thy kingdom may be preserved in peace...

In the Mishnah (Aboth III.2) it is said: 'Pray for the peace of the kingdom,' and this has always been the custom, both in Jewish and Christian worship, and still is today.

The *Amidah* Prayer, the Eighteen Blessings (in fact there are nineteen), which has already been mentioned, is said in every synagogue service; all the blessings except two are pre-Christian (the twelfth was added by Gamaliel II, about 100 A.D. and is against all heretics, including Christians, and the fifteenth was added a century later). Probably the original wording was shorter; the first three and the last three are always said daily throughout the year, the others are said on sabbaths and festivals and may give way to special prayers peculiar to the season or occasion. The first three and the last three must have been known off by heart by Jesus and his disciples and by the early Christians. They are, at least basically:

1. Blessed art Thou, O Lord our God, and the God of our fathers; the God of Abraham, the God of Isaac, and the God of Jacob. God most high who dost possess all things, blessed art Thou, O Lord, the Shield of Abraham.

2. Thou art mighty for ever, O Lord, that causest the wind to blow, and the rain to fall; Thou sustainest the living, Thou quickenest the dead.

49

3. Thou art Holy and holy is thy Name. And holy ones praise Thee every day. Blessed art Thou, O Lord, the Holy God.

17. Accept, O Lord our God, thy people Israel (here follows a prayer for the return of the 'oracle' and of the people to Zion; which is probably post A.D. 70) Blessed art Thou, O Lord, that restoreth thy Shekinah unto Zion. (This last also probably post A.D. 70.)

18. We give thanks unto Thee, O Lord our God and God of our fathers. Blessed art Thou, O Lord our God, good it is to praise Thee continually.

19. Give peace and blessing unto us, even unto Israel, thy people. Bless us all together, O Lord our God. Yea, it is good in thine eyes to bless thy people Israel. Blessed art Thou, O Lord, that blessest thy people with peace. Amen.

Another prayer which must have been familiar is the *Alenu* (meaning 'it is meet for us'), the prayer which now concludes morning prayer, and the *Kidushah* or Sanctification attached to the third benediction:

And one cried unto another and said, Holy, Holy, Holy is the Lord of Hosts, the whole earth is full of his glory; blessed be the glory of the Lord from his place; the Lord shall reign for ever, thy God, O Zion, unto all generations. Praise ye the Lord.

This 'sanctification' is so important that it occurs three times, in different parts of the liturgy.

Amen (so be it) is of course Hebrew; it is found in the psalms and was from the first the people's response in both temple and synagogue liturgy. In the *Amidah* prayer, at the end of each benediction the leader invited the response of the congregation 'and say ye all Amen', and it was also said at the end of the priestly blessing and at the end of each prayer; we are told that, in the great synagogue at Alexandria, where it was difficult to hear when a prayer ended, an official stood on a platform in the centre and waved a flag as a sign. 'Amen' is still used to end Jewish and Christian prayers.

The centre of Hebrew worship, both in temple and synagogue, was always the reading of and instruction in the Torah, to which were added the Prophets and the Writings and, in the synagogue, extracts from rabbinic treatises, while the Christians added their Gospels and their own sacred writings.

When we consider the pagan worship with which the Jews were surrounded, where the many gods were the embodiment of every human lust, magnified to 'godlike' proportions, it is not to be wondered at that many pagans attached themselves to Jewish synagogues. They might become proselytes, who accepted the whole Law, but there were also 'God-fearers' who believed and worshipped but who did not feel able to accept the full Law, especially the rite of circumcision; since this practice was utterly repugnant to Greeks.

Christianity offered the same high ideals: a single, unique God, creator of and supreme over all: a God of mercy and justice, who was holy. The Christian God demanded that his people should be holy, but did not demand of them that they outrage their ideals by what seemed to the Gentiles a mutilation of their bodies. These God-fearers, then, rapidly embraced the opportunity offered them. In St. Paul's epistles we can see how these pagans frequently strayed from the ideals put before them; but there was a firm Jewish moral and religious foundation and this kept the young Church faithful. We have inherited this moral and religious code from our Jewish ancestors.

7. Feasts and Fasts in New Testament Times

The three great pilgrimage feasts, when every male Israelite was obliged to present himself in the temple, were:

The Feast of Unleavened Bread, soon combined with The Passover (*Pasch*), in the spring: marking the beginning of the liturgical year;

The Feast of Weeks, (*Shavuoth*) sometimes called Pentecost, since it fell fifty days after Unleavened Bread, marking the completion of the cereal harvest;

The Feast of Tabernacles, or Booths, or Tents (*Succoth*), in the autumn; marking the beginning of the civil year, and the completion of the harvest.

Then there are the historical feasts:

Hanukkah (Dedication), in the winter, and

Purim (or Lots), in the spring.

And there are four historical fasts:

Tevet 10, which commemorates the beginning of the siege of Jerusalem in 586;

Tammuz 17, which commemorates the breach made in the wall;

Av 9: which commemorates the destruction of the first and second temples;

Tishri 3, called the Fast of Gedaliah, commemorating the murder of the viceroy appointed by Nebuchadnezzar:

and two minor fasts:

The Fast of Esther, held on Adar 13, and

The Fast of the Firstborn, kept on 14 Nisan, before Passover, commemorating God's sparing of the Israelites when He slew all the firstborn of the Egyptians;

To these must be added:

Rosh Hashannah (now New Year) and Yom Ha'atzmaut, the day when Israel celebrates her independence, and Tu B'shvat, the new year for trees.

These feasts and fasts illustrate Israel's keen sense of her unique history, mingling commemoration of events from the beginning with recent happenings.

The great fast of all is, of course, *Yom Kippur*, the Day of Atonement, when from sunset to sunset all Israel fasts and prays; this is still the very last obervance which a Jew will give up, for Leviticus XXIII. 29 says:

Whatsoever soul it be that shall not be afflicted (i.e. do penance and fast) in that same day he shall be cut off from his people.

Here we need concern ourselves only with six feasts, i.e. three pilgrim feasts and Hanukkah and Purim, with the great fast of Yom Kippur, since we know all these have existed in New Testament times; and Rosh Hashannah which, whether or not regarded as a New Year feast, was certainly kept as a major feast.

UNLEAVENED BREAD AND THE PASSOVER

Originally these two feasts were separate, and they are of different origin: unleavened bread is an agricultural feast, at the beginning of the new harvest season, and in the early calendars it alone is mentioned among the pilgrim feasts; passover is a nomadic feast, unique among Israel's feasts; perhaps it was the feast they sought permission to go from Egypt to celebrate:

And Moses and Aaron came, and said unto Pharoah, Thus saith the LORD, the God of Israel, Let my people go, that they may hold a feast unto me in the wilderness.

(Exodus V.1)

The lamb or kid was roasted (all other sacrifices were seethed) and in the ritual there is no suggestion of any kitchen utensils being used; the victim was roasted whole over a fire and must be consumed that same night. The ancient Arabs kept a similar feast. There is no priest and no altar and the meat is seasoned with bitter herbs (i.e. desert herbs which the nomads still use to season their bread) and unleavened bread (the usual bread of nomadic people) is eaten. The feast was celebrated at night, so a full moon was necessary, the 14/15 Nisan was therefore a suitable date; before the nomads set off from their winter to their summer pastures. And the painting of the lintels of the tents with blood was another nomad practice, to ward off evil spirits. Unleavened bread, *Matsoth*, was another feast, fixed for the 15th Nisan and kept for seven days; it was natural the two should be combined. The oldest calendars include unleavened bread with the other two pilgrim feasts, but do not mention Passover, which was kept at home. The first mention we have of the two being combined is in Ezekiel XLV.21:

> In the first month, in the fourteenth day of the month, ye shall
> have the passover, a feast of seven days; unleavened bread shall
> be eaten.

By New Testament times, of course, the two were inextricably linked; but the Passover remained a home festival; the lambs were sacrificed by the priests in the temple on the afternoon, then taken home and roasted and eaten that evening. Of all the Jewish feasts it is of course of primary importance for Christians, since the synoptic Gospel writers at least are convinced that it was at the passover seder (order of service) that Jesus instituted the Eucharist. It will therefore be worthwhile here to outline the order of the seder, service, an order which clearly lies behind the Gospel accounts.

The Passover Seder

This is the most important of all the passover services; it is held in the home and there is no reason to think that it differs substantially from the order which Jesus and his disciples would have observed, except that of course there is no longer any lamb; it is symbolically remembered by a roasted shankbone. At the head of the table, immediately in front of the celebrant, is the seder dish, containing three specially-baked *matsoth* (cakes of unleavened bread) and a hard-boiled egg (a symbol of eternal life), the shankbone and *charoseth* (a mixture of grated apples and almonds or nuts with raisins and cinnamon, and beside it a saucer with salt water and bitter herbs (horse radish or parsley).

The table is set with wine and goblets for each person; an extra goblet is provided for the prophet Elijah in case he arrives unexpectedly. The three unleavened cakes have this significance: the first two, the 'double portion' of manna gathered on the sabbath eve in the wilderness; and the third, the bread of poverty—affliction—eaten by Israel's forefathers as slaves in Egypt (Exodus XII.8); the *cheroseth*, on account of its brown colour, is to remind them of the bricks they made in Egypt, the shankbone, as has been said, is all that remains today of the paschal lamb, which Jesus would have eaten with his disciples, and the egg represents the free-will offering brought daily to the temple during the feast. During the seder, each person drinks four cups of wine; wine has always been symbolic in Israel of rejoicing. It must have been to arrange something like this, and to cook the lamb, that Jesus sent his disciples:

> And he sendeth two of his disciples, and saith unto them, Go into the city and...
>
> say to the goodman of the house, The master saith, where is the guest-chamber, where I shall eat the passover with my disciples?
>
> and he will shew you a large upper room furnished and ready: and there make ready for us...
>
> and they made ready the passover...
>
> And when it was evening he cometh with the twelve.
>
> (Mark XIV.13 ff)

The service opens with the sanctification of the meal, as does the sabbath meal held each Friday evening, by the celebrant i.e. the father of the family. The first cup of wine, called the *kiddush* or sanctification cup, is blessed and drunk by all. Then the celebrant washes his hands, to purify him for his priestly duties, and after he dips some parsley, or lettuce, in salt water and distributes it with a blessing, the company all partake. This represents the hyssop dipped in the blood of the lamb (Exodus XII.22) which marked the houses of the Hebrews in Egypt, when the angel of death smote all the firstborn of the Egyptians. Then the celebrant breaks in two the middle *Matsoth*, leaving one half on the seder dish and placing the other half aside as the *afikomen* or dessert. This custom is thought by some to have its origin in the reservation of a portion of the paschal lamb, which will be eaten at the end of the meal, as the last morsel. Then the seder dish is taken hold of by the whole company, who elevate it, saying:

> This is the bread of affliction which our fathers ate in the land of Egypt. Let all who are hungry come in and celebrate the Passover.

These words, which now conclude with the words 'this year here − next year in the Land of Israel; this year as slaves − next year free!' are said in Aramaic, and date from the early Roman period; it is reasonable to think that the first part at least goes back to New Testament times.

The youngest child present now asks questions concerning the meaning of this night as distinguished from other nights. One of the questions is: 'Why though on other nights we take our meal sitting, at this meal we all recline' (Cf. John XIII.23). The questions give rise to the *Haggadah* (telling forth) in narrative form, with comments, stories and explanations, of Israel's slavery in Egypt, the Exodus and the birth of the nation. This is followed by an outburst of praise in the recitation of the first part of the *Hallel* (Psalm CXIII and Psalm CXIV) and the drinking of the second, the *Haggadah* cup of wine. Then all wash their hands in preparation for eating the meal (in the days of the temple of course the paschal lamb) which is to follow.

The celebrant then breaks the first and second of the unleavened cakes and distributes pieces to all present; these are eaten after the recitation of the blessing. A piece of horse-radish (the bitter herb) is dipped in *cheroseth* and also distributed to and eaten by each person. The evening meal is then served.

It is scarcely necessary to point out the parallels in this ritual with the Gospel accounts of the Last Supper: the explanation of the meaning of the meal, the washing of the disciples' feet, the blessing, breaking and distribution of the bread and wine, the sanctification of the cup and the dipping of the bitter herbs in the *cheroseth* followed by the distribution of the 'morsel' to the company. It is interesting to note that in Mark and Matthew the bread is distributed first, whereas Luke puts the blessing of the cup before that of the bread, suggesting that some of the early Christian Churches associated the eucharistic cup with the first, the *Kiddush* cup, and others connected it with the third cup, drunk 'after supper' (cf. 1 Corinthians XI.25) Those used to Christian ritual will find many more parallels which have survived into the eucharistic liturgies of their respective churches.

At the conclusion of the meal, the piece of bread which was reserved, as the *afikomen* is distributed, grace is said and the third cup, the 'cup of blessing' (1 Corinthians X.16) is drunk.

The door is then opened (presumably to allow guests who have come from far to leave; the ritual which follows this nowadays dates from the Middle Ages). Then the fourth cup of wine is filled and drunk and the second part of the Hallel (Psalms XV to XVIII) is sung; cf. the conclusion of the Last Supper:

And when they had sung a hymn, they went out unto the Mount of Olives.

(Mark XIV.26)

The synagogue has a festival service in the evening, which many Jews attend before the Passover Seder, a service with additions next morning, and the festival lasts for seven days; as that of Unleavened Bread always did.

The *Pasch* (Passover) is essentially a time of family rejoicing and remembrance: old friendships are renewed, hospitality is exercised widely and racial bonds are consolidated. The lamb was sacrificed on the afternoon of 14 Nisan and eaten that evening, the beginning of 15 Nisan (called *Abid* in the biblical calendar; see Exodus XIII.4). From now until 21 Nisan only unleavened bread may be eaten, and indeed no old leaven may remain in the house from before the feast.

The synoptic gospels limit Jesus' ministry to one year, (perhaps for liturgical convenience) but in John's gospel we see him attending at least three passover feasts, and it is at passover time that he takes the opportunity to give his teaching on the Bread of Life. (John VI.4 and 35 ff).

PENTECOST, ALSO KNOWN AS THE FEAST OF WEEKS OR SHAVUOTH

The Counting of the Omer

The interval between Passover and Pentecost is known as 'The Days of the Counting.' The *omer* here is a measure, about half a gallon, of barley (Exodus XVI.36); but the title is misleading, since what is counted are the days, fifty, between Passover and Pentecost. It is the time of the cereal harvest, beginning with barley and ending with wheat, which lasted seven weeks in Palestine. The counting, which was originally done in the temple, was and still is done in the synagogue. It is preceeded by a blessing:

> Blessed art thou... who hast sanctified us by thy commandments and hast commanded us to count the days of the omer... this is the... day since the omer.

After a week, the number of weeks are also counted until forty-nine days are reached; the fiftieth is the Feast of Pentecost. So it is celebrated on Sivan 6 and 7; in Exodus XXIII.16 it is called the Feast of the Harvest, though this is misleading to us since the great Harvest Festival is Succoth, when the grape and olive harvests have also been gatheried in; a less misleading title today is the name given it in Numbers XXVIII.26, The Day of the First Fruits. The synagogue is decorated with trees, plants and flowers, and Jewish homes are similarly decorated.

The Feast is also regarded by the Jews as the Feast of revelation, the Feast of the giving of the Law, because of the tradition that the law-giving on Sinai took place on the sixth day of the third month (i.e. Sivan). The book of Jubilees puts all giving of covenants, from Noah onwards, on the Feast of Weeks and it was the most important of the feasts for the Qumran community; for the rabbis, however, it was of secondary importance and that it was the date of the giving of the law was not accepted by them until the second century A.D. However, the idea must have been current in New Testament times,

58

and it seems reasonable to link it with the coming of the Holy Spirit, the spirit of truth, on Pentecost. Today these two ideas are linked in the readings for the feast:

On the first day: Exodus XIX to XXII, the account of the law- giving on Sinai; and Ezekiel I, the relevation of God's glory.

On the second day: Deuteronomy XV.19 to XVI.17, the offering of firstlings etc. and Habakkuk III, known as 'Habakkuk's Psalm', again exalting God's majesty, and The Book of Ruth, which has been called 'A Harvest Idyll.'

This, then, was the second of the great Pilgrim Feasts, and accounts for Jerusalem being full of Jews from all over the Diaspora, at the time when the Holy Spirit descended on the disciples at Pentecost (Acts II.5 ff).

THE NEW YEAR – ROSH HASHANAH

This is one of the great feasts among the Jews and was already so in New Testament times and the Mishnah has a special treatise on it. It is kept on 1 Tishri; which would be the seventh month in a calendar beginning in the Spring. The *shofar* (horn) was blown, hymns of praise sung. Under this name and with these rites, it is never mentioned in the Old Testament: neither in liturgical texts nor in pre-exilic texts nor in Ezra nor Nehemiah. The only time the name occurs is in Ezekiel XL.1:

In the beginning of the year i.e. *rosh hashanah* 'the head of the year.'

But this is the beginning of a year which began in the spring; Ezekiel is referring to Nisan, not Tishri when Rosh Hashanah was later kept. This change of calendar is emphasized in Exodus XII.2:

This month (Abib, later called Nisan) shall be unto you the beginning of the months: it shall be the first month of the year to you.

But the confusion of the calendars has already been dealt with and it is clear that in the New Testament the beginning of the year, at any rate for some purposes, was reckoned to be 1 Tishri.

Two texts, belonging to the final edition of the Pentateuch, later than Ezra and Nehemiah, are of interest: Leviticus XXIII. 24 to 25 says:

> And the LORD spake unto Moses, saying,
>
> Speak unto the children of Israel, saying, In the seventh month, on the first day of the month, shall be a solemn rest unto you, a memorial of blowing of trumpets,an holy convocation.
>
> Ye shall do no servile work; and ye shall offer an offering made by fire unto the LORD

Numbers XXIX. 1 to 6 says much the same in a more extended form; It calls the feast the Day of Acclamation and lays down what sacrifices are to be offered; but it is not clear from either text that the feast was to be regarded as a New Year feast. It seems to be simply an especially solemn New Moon feast. At the time the first of the month was a usual day for festivals and Tishri is full of them: The Day of Atonement on 10th and Succoth from 15 th to 22nd, and it perhaps commemorated the old new year which began, for both religious and civil purposes, in the autumn, at about the Feast of Succoth. Josephus does not include it among the list of Jewish Feasts; Philo mentions ten Jewish feasts, among which 1 Tishri is a Feast of Trumpets at the beginning of the month of great feasts.

It is impossible, therefore, to say at what time and in what circumstances this feast became a New Year feast—it must have been at some time between the final recension of the Pentateuch, in the second century B.C. and the completion of the Mishnah in the second century A.D. But it was clearly before this an important feast, and since it is connected with the Day of Atonement and leads on to Succoth it cannot be omitted here.

It is sometimes known as *Yom Teruah*, The Day of the Shofar-Blowing. On ordinary new moon celebrations the shofar was blown when the sacrifices for the day were offered, but on Yom Teruah the blowing is continuous. The shofar, still used, is a ram's horn, without a mouthpiece, 'sharply bent at the broad side near the base, to double the current of air.' It emits a very primitive, ear-splitting sound and is very difficult to perform on successfully; if the performer is chosen principally for his piety rather than his blowing ability the result can be 'peculiar'; its effect is always 'soul-shattering.' It is intended to remind the worshippers of:

1. Creation
2. Their duty to return to God
3. God's revelation at Sinai
4. The exhortations of the prophets
5. The destruction of the Temple
6. The binding of Isaac for sacrifice
7. Imminent danger
8. The Day of Judgment
9. The redemption of Israel
10. The Resurrection

St. Paul obviously knew this last significance of the trumpet-blowing:

> In a moment, in the twinkling of an eye, at the last trump: for the trumpet shall sound, and the dead shall be raised...
>
> (I Cor.XV.52)

The main intention is to call men to repentance, it also serves to carry to God's throne the cry that evokes his grace and mercy. This is brought out in the prayer said before the shofar is blown for the first time:

> Thou hast aforetime heard my voice, O hide not thine ear at my breathing, at my cry. May it please Thee, O Lord my God, the God of Judgment, that now be an acceptable time before Thee, and that thou in the multitude of thy mercies and loving-kindness wilt vouchsafe to rend all the veils which mark a separation this day between Thee and thy people, Israel, and send away all who slander and reproach us. Shut the mouth of Satan, that he accuse us not, for on Thee our eyes are hanging. I will exult Thee, my God, my King, the God of Judgment. Hear the voice of the prayers and the teru'oth (i.e. the trumpet-blowings) of Israel, thy people, this day, in mercy. Amen.

Other names for the feast are: The Feast of Trumpets, or The Day of Memorial (*Yom Zikkaron*), or The Day of Judgment (*Yom ha Din*), each emphasizing a different aspect of the season.

As has been said, in the Amidah prayer (The Eighteen Blessings), the first three and the last three are fixed, but the middle ones are peculiar to the season; those for Rosh Hashanah give the peculiar flavour of the festival. They come under three headings:

Kingdoms: containing verses of Scripture in which God's goodness and greatness are recognized and they ask his blessing, beginning: 'But on account of our sins we were exiled from our land...'

Remembrances: which is made up of verses in which God is shown to be mindful of mankind, and especially of Israel, and

Horn-Blowings: which is made up of verses in which the shofar is literally or metaphorically named, in passages where God, as it were sounds in thunder notes a call to Israel and to all mankind.

Of the three, Remembrances is the most striking; it begins: 'Thou rememberest...' and gives the feast it special character of *Yom ha Din*, The Day of Judgment, reflecting the belief that God has chosen this day and those connected with it as a special time of passing judgment on his creatures.

The Amidah concludes with forty-four petitions beginning: 'Our Father, our King...'; these contain some striking parallels to clauses in the Lord's Prayer:

Our Father, our King, we have sinned before Thee.
Our Father, our King, we have none other King but Thee.
Our Father, our King, renew for us a good year.
Our Father, our King, bring us back before Thee in perfect repentance.
Our Father, our King, vouchsafe to write us in the Book of Redemption.
Our Father, our King, hear us, though no good works of our own are in us.
We will sanctify also thy Name throughout the world.
O God, the God of our fathers, reign Thou over the whole world in thy glory.

It is worth noting, by the way, that there is no clause in the Lord's Prayer which is not found in the Old Testament; its uniqueness lies in the way in which they are brought together:

After this manner therefore pray ye:
Our Father which art in heaven,
Hallowed be thy name,
Thy kingdom come

Thy will be done as in heaven so on earth.
Give us this day our daily bread
And forgive us our debt, as we also have forgiven our debtors,
And bring us not into temptation;
But deliver us from the evil one.

The belief that at this time God judged his creatures doubtless persuaded the synagogue to give the first ten days of the year a penitential character. According to Jewish tradition the great Books of Judgment are opened on 1 Tishri and closed ten days later, on Yom Kippur, The Day of Atonement.

According to the Targum (the rabbinic commentary) on Job 1.6 ff., the scene there described took place on New Year's Day; Satan yearly plays his part of accuser before the divine judge. In the Targum it is said that the sounds of the shofar are intended to 'confuse' Satan. Three books are opened: one for the throroughly wicked, one for the thoroughly pious and the third for the large, intermediate class. The fate of the first two is decided on the spot, that of the intermediate is suspended till the Day of Atonement, when every man's fate is sealed.

God, seated on his throne to judge the world, openeth the Book of Records, it is read, every man's name being inscribed therein.

The great trumpet is sounded, the angels shudder, saying: 'This is the Day of Judgment', for his very ministers are not pure before God.

As a shepherd mustereth his flock, so does God cause every living soul to pass before Him to fix the limit of every creature's life and to fore-ordain its destiny. On New Year's Day the decree is written, on The Day of Atonement it is sealed, who shall live and who shall die, etc. But penitence, prayer and charity may avert the evil decree.

The fate not only of individuals but also of countries is determined at the same time: which are destined to the sword, which to peace, which to famine, which to plagues.

This feast, and the Fast of the Day of Atonement linked with it, are not mentioned in the New Testament. The Christian Church transferred the great time of penance to Good Friday and the preceding days of penance to the Fast of Lent. But Jesus and his disciples must have attended temple and synagogue on Rosh Hashannah and on Yom Kippur; it is not known how the earliest Christians reconciled these days with their belief in the atoning efficacy of Jesus' death, but Jesus himself shows his knowledge of and belief in the 'Book of Records' at least symbolically:

> Howbeit, in this rejoice not, that the spirits are subject unto you; but rejoice that your names are written in heaven.
>
> (Luke X.20)

A man's fate is determined according as merit or demerit predominates in the final reckoning; so it is necessary to lay up a multitude of good deeds before the Day of Atonement. Those emerging successful are entered in the Book of Life. This is the meaning of Moses' prayer, for the sinful people, when he states that if God will not forgive them then he too will forego mercy with the people:

> Yet now, if thou wilt forgive their sin—; and if not blot me, I pray thee, out of thy book which thou hast written.
>
> (Exodus XXXII.32)

There are numerous references to this Book of Life in both the Old and New Testaments: e.g. Isaiah IV.3; Psalm LXIX.28; Daniel XII.1; Philippians IV.3; Revelation V.5. This explains the petition: 'Inscribe us in the Book of Life' and the Jewish salutation on New Year's Eve: 'May you be inscribed (i.e. in the Book of Life) for a happy year.'

But this is not only a time of judgment; it is also a time of remembrance of God's mercies in the past and his gracious promises for the future. Various reminiscences are summed up in the remembrance of God's work in creation, accomplished at this season; this memorial proclaims the world's creator as King, recalls the delivery of Israel from Egypt and remembers the giving of the Law on Sinai when 'the trumpet sounded long;'

There is a memorial also of the binding of Isaac—the patriarchal type of the future resurrection, imploring the goodwill of the heavenly Father such as that which Abraham's faithful submission and obedience evoked, when he withheld not his only son.

And there are memorials of the divinely-promised return of Israel to Jerusalem, and the rebuilding of the Holy City (presumably dating from after A.D. 70) the coming of the Messiah and the resurrection of the dead.

There is a custom observed at this time by many Jews who visit the graves of their dead, offering prayers and salutations at their last earthly resting place. It used to be a custom among some German evangelical Christians, on the last Sunday in Advent to wear mourning for their dead who had died during the year and to remember them in their services; the Christian feasts of All Saints and all Souls fall on 1st and 2nd November, respectively. All of this witnesses to a human instinct to remember, towards the end of the year, those who have died during it. Advent of course is the beginning of the Christian year. It begins the year with four weeks of preparation, which have sometimes taken on a penitential character, but not like that of the weeks of Lent; since Advent celebrates 'coming', the coming of the Saviour.

The dedication of the first ten days of the year to repentance is haggadistically (i.e. in the rabbinic explanation) connected with the command in Exodus XXXIV.26:

> The firstfruits of thy ground thou shalt bring into the house of the LORD thy God...

Here once more we see the confusion caused by the change in the calendar; 'firstfruits' refer to a year beginning in Nisan, the cereal harvest, but it is being related to a New Year beginning in Tishri, towards the end of the grape and olive harvest; but seeing this instruction as referring to new year the rabbis regarded the first ten days of the year as an offering (of first fruits) to the Lord.

How far this account of the feast accords with what Jesus and his disciples experienced we have no way of telling. But we must bear in mind the tendency of liturgy, especially a liturgy having such an elaborate ritual as the Jewish, not to change radically and to develop only very slowly, according to the needs of the time. We may, therefore, I think, assume that this account, in outline, of what takes place in a modern synagogue gives us a fair approximation of what they must have known.

The same caution must be applied to the account of Yom Kippur, which follows: although here we are on safer ground since the ritual to be observed in the temple is outlined in Leviticus XVI.

YOM KIPPUR THE DAY OF ATONEMENT

The observance of Yom Kippur is the very last religious practice a Jew gives up; even if he neglects all other religious observances he will make an effort to observe this day. Its ritual belongs to the last days of the Old Testament and by New Testament times it was sufficiently important to be called simply 'The Day' without further qualification. It has always been observed on 10 Tishri. It is mentioned in Leviticus XXIII.27 to 32 and in Numbers XXIX. 7 to 11, which are both late texts and its ritual is described in Leviticus XVI, which is also late.

No work must be done on this day; instead penance and fasting, from sunset on 9 Tishri, when the Day begins, to sunset on the 10th must be strictly observed. The people met in the temple, though this is not one of the pilgrim feasts, where sacrifice was offered in expiation for the sins of priests and people and for the cleansing of the temple and the altar. The ritual described in Leviticus XVI shows several strata and has been much re- edited. It is composed of two ceremonies, different in spirit and origin: the first is a levitical ritual in which the high priest offered a bull for his own sins and those of his 'house' (the Aaronic priesthood) he then entered behind the veil of the Holy of Holies, for the only time in the year, to incense the mercy seat and to sprinkle it with the bull's blood. After this he offered a goat for the sins of the people and took this blood, too, behind the veil, where he sprinkled it over the mercy seat. This expiation of the sins of the priesthood and the people is linked with an expiation for the sanctuary and particularly for the altar, where blood was sprinkled and rubbed; ideas about purity and the expiatory value of blood are characteristic of Leviticus. The two ceremonies are combined in the summing-up at the end of the chapter: 'And he shall make atonement for the holy sanctuary.' This does not mean that the 'sanctuary' was thought to have sinned; verse 16 has said, 'he shall make atonement for the holy place, because of the uncleanness of the children of Israel, and because of their transgressions, even all their sins.'

> And he shall make atonement for the tent of meeting, and for the altar, and he shall make atonement for the priests and for all the people of the assembly.
>
> And this shall be an everlasting statute unto you, to make atonement for the children of Israel because of all their sins once in the year.
>
> (Leviticus XVI.33,34)

Into this ritual another, based on other ideas, has been inserted. The community put forward two goats and lots were cast: one was 'for Yahweh' the other 'for Azazel.' The goat chosen for Yahweh was sacrificed for the sins of the people, as already described, then the other goat, alive, was 'set before Yahweh' and the high priest placed his hands on its head and transferred to it all the faults, deliberate or indeliberate, of the Israelites; a man then took it into the desert and it took with it all the sins of the people. Rabbinic tradition says it was taken to Beth Hadudun, the modern Kirbeth Kareidan, overlooking the Kidron Valley, about three-and-a-half miles from Jerusalem, where it was cast over the cliffs. This is the 'scape-goat' of the English Bible, but the LXX and the Vulgate call it the 'goat sent out' and in Hebrew it is destined 'for Azazel'; this was probably the name of a devil, the desert was thought of as the dwelling-place of devils. But the goat is *not* sacrificed to Azazel; the transfer of sins to it and their expiation is only effective because the goat has first been presented to Yahweh. Once it had become charged with the sins of the people it became impure and could not be sacrificed so it had to be sent away; the man who took it away also became impure until the evening. The origin of this custom, or how it became incorporated into the ritual, is not known.

This combination of levitical custom with popular superstition is another characteristic of very late ritual in the Old Testament; but we cannot say when it was instituted. The remission of sins is for the community rather than for individuals, so as to cleanse Yahweh's land from any residual taint of individual sins that may have remained even after legal and ritual purification had been undergone. Only so could the nation and community preserve the ceremonial purity which would allow Yahweh to live in their midst.

When the temple and its ritual were destroyed the Jews refused to consider the Day of Atonement as done away with. No religious ceremony is more fondly cherished even by modern Jews.

The rabbis taught that 'charity or repentance' was an accepted substitute for sacrifice and with this an atoning efficacy was conveyed to the day itself. 'At this time when there is no temple there is no atonement but repentance. Repentance atones for all transgressions; even though a man be wicked all his days, none of his wickedness is accounted to him, for it is said: "As for the wickedness of the wicked, he shall not fall thereby in the day that he turneth from his wickedness" (Ezekiel XXXIII.12). The Day itself, duly observed, is also seen in itself to atone for those who repent, for it is said: 'For on that Day he shall make atonement for you' (Leviticus XVI.30). But the rabbis rightly insisted on the necessity of true, deep, heartfelt repentance; according to the Mishnah, repentance atones for light offences then and there, God pardons them immediately. With heavy offences repentance makes them hang in the balance until The Day comes and atones for them. So in grave offences The Day itself, duly observed, is necessary for divine forgiveness, though this implies no more than a formal suspension of forgiveness between repentance and The Day. But there is danger here of assigning superstitious efficacy to this particular day, and the rabbis are conscious of this. The Mishnah stresses that the ceremonies of The Day of Atonement are useless without repentance: 'Death and the Day of Atonement work atonement where there is repentance' and 'if a man says "I will sin and repent, I will sin and repent" heaven does not give him the means of practising repentance; and if he says: "I will sin and the Day of Atonement will bring atonement" The Day of Atonement will bring him no atonement.'

In another Mishnah passage it says: 'The Day of Atonement absolves for sins against God but not for sins against a fellow man until his companion is reconciled.' So it is customary to terminate all feuds on the eve of The Day. Even the souls of the dead are included in the community of those pardoned on The Day of Atonement; so it is customary for children to have public mention made in the synagogue and to make charitable donations on behalf of parents' souls on The Day. But no amount of charity will avail the soul of the persistently wicked man.

There are five synagogue services on this day: evening prayer, on the evening of 9th, and the next day morning prayer, an additional morning prayer (the *Musaf*) afternoon prayer and the closing prayer; in fact prayer is held continuously throughout 10 Tishri. Even in reformed synagogues today, prayer is practically continuous throughout the day. This used to be so in Christian communities on Good Friday and is still the practice wherever practicable in enclosed monastic communities.

The structure of the prayers follows that of ordinary days with modifications and additions; the most important alterations affect the Amidah Prayer and the additions are chiefly penitential prayers and forms of confession. The part in which the characteristic note of The Day receives fullest and most intense expression is the central benediction said in the amidah prayer in the Musaf (additional morning prayer). This paragraph, which occupies seventy-two pages in the festal prayer book, begins with a beautiful prayer for the blessing of the synagogue reader. Then follows a summary account of biblical history from Adam to Aaron; the whole temple service of the Day of Atonement is then described, including the three forms of confession used by the high priest for himself, his household and the people; in each of the three confessions he pronounced the ineffable Name of Yahweh, at which the congregation 'knelt and prostrated themselves, falling on their faces and saying: "Blessed be the Name of his glorious majesty for ever and ever." After the description of his sacrificial duties a composition described as the prayer of the high priest, offered by him on the successful completion of the sacrifices, is made. Then follows a rapturous description of the beauty of the high priest, based on Ecclesiasticus XLVI ff. The lines are chanted by the reader and closed in each case by a refrain said by the congregation.

The most characteristic note of the day, however, is struck in the various confessions of sin (*widduy*), and these may well go back to temple times. The most frequent is the one attached to the amidah prayer for each service, beginning:

> Our God, and God of our fathers, let our prayer come before Thee; hide not Thyself from our supplication, for we are not arrogant and stiff-necked, that we should say before Thee, O Lord our God and God of our fathers, we are righteous and have not sinned. Yea, indeed, truly, we have sinned.

> We have trespassed, we have been faithless, we have robbed, we have spoken basely, we have committed iniquity, we have

wrought unrighteousness, we have been presumptuous, we have done violence, we have forged lies, we have counselled evil, we have spoken falsely, we have scoffed, we have revolted, we have blasphemed, we have been rebellious, we have acted perversely, we have transgressed, we have persecuted, we have been stiff-necked, we have done wickedly, we have corrupted ourselves, we have committed abomination, we have gone astray and we have led astray.

May it then by thy good will, O Lord our God and God of our fathers, to forgive us for all our sins, to pardon us for all our iniquities, and to grant remission of all our transgressions; for the sin which we have committed before Thee, under compulsion, or of our free will,

And in the sin we have committed before Thee in hardening of the heart;

And in the sin we have committed...(there follow forty-four clauses, then):

For all these O God of forgiveness, forgive us, pardon us, grant us remission.

Prayers like these would seem to fill out the temple sacrifices and bear witness to the repentance which the rabbis always taught was individually necessary, even in the days of the temple, before The Day could prove efficacious for the worshippers.

THE FEAST OF SUCCOTH—TABERNACLES

The Jewish Harvest Festival

This is the third of the great pilgrimage feasts; it is the most important and was the most crowded of the three annual pilgrimages to Jerusalem: Leviticus XXIII.39 calls it 'The Feast of Yahweh':

Howbeit on the fifteenth day of the seventh month, when ye have gathered in the fruits of the land, ye shall keep the feast of the LORD seven days; on the first day shall be a solemn rest, and on the eighth day shall be a solemn rest.

And you shall take you on the first day the fruit of goodly trees, branches of palm trees, and boughs of thick trees, and willows of the brook; and ye shall rejoice before the LORD your God seven days.

And ye shall keep it a feast unto the LORD seven days in the year: it is a statute for ever in your generations: ye shall keep it in the seventh month.

Ye shall dwell in booths seven days; all that are homeborn in Israel shall dwell in booths;

That your generation may know that I made the children of Israel to dwell in booths, when I brought them out of the land of Egypt; I am the LORD your God.

(Leviticus XXIII.39 to 43)

Deuteronomy XVI.13 calls it *Succoth* (Tabernacles in the English translation). It is also sometimes called Tents or Booths. It is pre-eminently a feast of rejoicing, as our English harvest festival or American Thanksgiving is. It was on this feast that Elkanah went up to Shiloh, taking with him his two wives, and when Eli saw Hannah, he first reproved her and then encouraged her to hope for fulfilment:

And it came to pass as she (Hannah) continued praying before the LORD, that Eli marked her mouth.

Now Hannah, she spoke in her heart; only her lips moved, but her voice was not heard; therefore Eli thought that she was drunken... And Hannah answered and said, No, my lord, I am a woman of a sorrowful spirit...I poured out my soul before the LORD... Eli..said, Go in peace: and the God of Israel grant thy petition that thou hast asked of him...

And it came to pass, when the time was come about, that Hannah conceived, and bore a son; and she called his name Samuel..

(1 Samuel I.12 to 20)

In due course Hannah brought Samuel up to Shiloh to conse-crate him to the Lord, and it was then that she uttered her great thanksgiving which was surely in Mary and Elizabeth's minds when Mary, or Elizabeth, or both antiphonally, intoned for the first time the Magnificat: so frequently used in Christian worship.

And Hannah prayed and said: Mine heart exulteth in the LORD, mine horn is exalted in the LORD...I rejoice in thy salvation.

There is none holy as the LORD; for there is none beside thee: neither is there any rock like our God.

71

Talk no more so exceeding proudly; let not arrogancy come out of your mouth: for the LORD is a God of knowledge, and by him actions are weighed.

The bows of the mighty are broken, and they that stumbled are girded with strength.

They that were full have hired themselves out for bread; and they that were hungry have ceased: (i.e. have ceased to be hungry) yea the barren have borne seven, and she that hath many children languisheth.

The LORD killeth and maketh alive: he brings down to the grave and bringeth up.

The Lord maketh poor and maketh rich: he bringeth low and he also lifteth up.

He raiseth up the poor out of the dust, he lifteth up the needy from the dunghill, to make them sit with princes and inherit the throne of glory:(1 Samuel II.1 to 8)

The Magnificat

My soul doth magnify the LORD
And my spirit hath rejoiced in God my Saviour.
For he hath looked upon the low estate of his handmaiden:
For behold from henceforth all generations shall call me blessed.
For he that is mighty hath done to me great things;
And holy is his name.
And his mercy is unto generations and generations
Of them that fear him.
He hath shewed strength with his arm;
He hath scattered the proud in the imagination of their heart.
He hath put down princes from their thrones,
And hath exalted them of low degree.
The hungry he hath filled with good things;
And the rich he hath sent empty away.
He hath holpen Israel his servant,
That he might remember mercy
(As he spake unto our fathers)
Towards Abraham and his seed for ever.

(Luke I.46ff)

Even in Josephus' time this was 'the holiest and the greatest of Hebrew feasts' (*Antiquities* VIII.iv.1) so we may presume it to have been of similar importance in New Testament times.

Originally it was the farmers' feast, the harvest festival, when all the produce of the fields was gathered in:

> The feast of ingathering, at the end of the year, when thou gatherest in thy labours out of the field.
> (Exodus XXIII.16)

and all the produce of the threshing-floor and the presses:

> Thou shalt keep the feast of tabernacles seven days, after that thou hast gathered in from thy threshing-floor and from thy wine-press.
> (Deuteronomy XVI.13)

When all the fruits of the earth had been gathered, and the olives and grapes pressed, the farmers assembled to give God thanks; as the Jews still do and as Christians too do at their harvest festivals.

The feast is first mentioned in detail in Deuteronomy XVI.13 to 15, where it is called *Succoth* (Tabernacles) and described as one of the pilgrimage feasts; it lasted seven days, Leviticus XXIII.36 mentions an eighth day which shall be one of solemn assembly when sacrifices are to be offered. But in all the mentions of the feast, the eighth day is regarded as an addition, an appendix to the seven-day feast. In modern Israel the feast also lasts seven days, beginning on 15 Tishri (five days after the Day of Atonement), the first day is a full festival the rest half-holidays, but the eighth day is again a full festival, followed on the ninth day by the feast of *Simchat Torah* (Rejoicing in the Law), which is not a feast legislated for in the Bible and therefore not mentioned again here.

Later, but still in biblical times, the feast, like other Jewish feasts, acquired an historical significance: the people were to live for the seven days in booths, in memory of their sojourn in tents in the desert. This is laid down in the passage quoted above from Leviticus, though in the Mishnah, in its later ritual, there is no mention of living in booths, the only rule is that the people must remain in Jerusalem. II Chronicles VII.8 tells us that Solomon kept the feast for seven days and on the eighth day held a solemn assembly after which 'he sent the people away unto their tents.' Nehemiah VIII refers to the re- introduction of the feast under Ezra:

And they found written in the law how that the LORD had commanded by Moses, that the children of Israel should dwell in booths in the feast of the seventh month...

that they should...Go forth unto the mount, and fetch olive branches, and branches of wild olive, and myrtle branches, and palm branches, and branches of thick trees, to make booths...

So the people went forth, and brought them, and made themselves booths, every one upon the roof of his house, and in their courts, and in the courts of the house of God, and in the broad place of the water gate, and in the broad place of the gate of Ephraim.

And all the congregation of them that were come again out of captivity made booths, and dwelt in the booths:
(Nehemiah VIII.14 to 17)

The 'fruit of goodly trees, branches of palm trees and boughs of thick trees, and willows of the brook' of the Leviticus passage are not intended for the building of the booths, they are carried round in joyous procession; this we know from 2 Maccabees X. 6 ff where the re-dedication of the temple is said to have been celebrated 'as in the feast of the tabernacles': 'they bare branches, and fair boughs, and palms also, and sang psalms.' Josephus tells us how the citizens pelted the hated high priest and king, Alexander Janneus, with the citrons which they carried in their hands (*Antiquities* XIII,xiv.5). The ritual described in the Mishnah says that a citron (*ethrog*) and a palm branch (*lulab*) were carried, one in each hand: branches of myrtle and willow were tied to the stem of the lulab. The modern feast is kept in much the same way, so we may be reasonably assured that it was similarly kept in New Testament times, though we have no instances of the people living in booths; as is the custom today. Every Jew with a garden or court builds a lightly constructed booth and lives, or at any rate has meals in it, while the feast lasts. The booths are adorned with fruits, flowers and leaves, as are booths constructed in synagogues. On the first evening the meal, like that of the weekly Sabbath, is preceded with *Kiddush*, i.e. a solemn sanctification over a cup of wine, which is handed round, of which all drink, and two wheaten loaves are provided of which each partakes. The Kiddush is repeated on the eighth day, at the end of the feast.

In the synagogue the ancient character of the feast, that of the ingathering of the fruits of the harvest is emphasized. The synagogue is decorated with harvest fruits and flowers, as our churches are for our harvest festival, and there are palm-branch processions.

The worshipper takes the lulab in his right hand and the ethrog in his left and recites the following blessings:

> Blessed art thou, O Lord our god, King of the universe, who hast sanctified us with thy commandments and commanded us to take up the palm branch.
> Blessed art thou, O Lord our God, King of the universe, who hast preserved us alive, sustained us and brought us to enjoy this season.

The branches are lifted during the recitation of the Hallel (Psalms CXIII to CXVIII) during morning prayer. These ceremonies will recall to many Christians ceremonies in our churches on Palm Sunday, when we are commemorating the Jewish crowd's welcome to Jesus on his entry into Jerusalem before his passion.

Each day in the synagogue there is a Musaf (an additional service which follows morning prayer) as on Sabbaths and holy days. At the end of the Musaf the scroll of the Law is taken out of the ark and carried to the reading desk, a procession of worshippers, each with lulub and ethrog, is formed and circles while *hoshanahs* are recited, introduced by:

> For thy sake, O our God, save now! (i.e. Hoshanah!)
> For thy sake, O our Creator, save now!
> For our sake, O our Redeemer, save now!
> For thy sake, O thou who seekest us, save now!

Hoshanah is the Hebrew for 'Save now!' but it is all to easy for Christians, used to singing 'Hosannah in the highest' to forget that this is Israel's ancient cry against her oppressors. British soldiers who took part in the Occupation of Palestine after the 1939–45 war tell us of their dread of hearing the tramp of marching feet to the chant of 'Hoshanah!' knowing that it signalled another Israeli rising and more bloodshed. Doubtless Greek and Roman troops heard the same, during their occupation of the land, and it is reasonable to think that Jesus and his apostles and the early Christians heard, and participated in similar chants.

Every day of the feast is provided with this additional Musaf Service and with processions, culminating on the final day, The Feast of *Hoshana Rabba* (The Great Hoshannah). At the completion of the processions the worshippers return to their places, the palm branch is laid aside and a small bunch of five willow twigs tied together (called a 'hoshannah' since it is peculiar to this feast) is taken up; hymns, especially hymns calling for the coming of the Messiah are sung; unfortunately we know of none dating from New Testament times. Then a petition is made for the forgiveness of sins and each worshipper shakes or strikes the willow-branch until the leaves fall and it is thrown away.

Although we do not know precisely how the synagogue services were conducted in New Testament times, we know that the waving of the palm-branches and the citrons and the Hoshanah ceremonies are survivals from the great ceremonies connected with the water-drawing during the Feast of Tabernacles in the time of the temple. A golden pitcher containing three *logs* (a log equals about three-quarters of a pint) was filled by the high priest with water from the Pool of Siloam and brought through the Water Gate into the Temple, the multitude meanwhile reciting Isaiah XII.3ff: 'Therefore with joy shall ye draw water out of the wells of salvation…' Amid trumpet blasts the water, with a libation of wine, was poured into a funnel in the altar through which the mingled liquids flowed down to the Kedron Brook by an underground passage.

The season was one of great festivity, especially on the evening of the first day when, in the brilliantly-lit Court of the Women there was a Torah dance, in which leading Israelites took part, to the accompaniment of singing and music, lasting till early morning.

The libation of water is probably to be accounted for by the ancient practice of making a libation as a sign to encourage rain, which is closely associated with the Feast of Tabernacles since this is the time when the Land of Israel expects its rainy period, on which its next harvest depends. Of this ceremony and its accompaniments the Mishnah says: 'He who has not seen the joy of the water-drawing has never seen joy in his life.' During the feast the libation of water was made each day at the time of the morning sacrifice. It is to this custom that Jesus is referring in John VII.37 ff:

Now on the last day, the great day of the feast, Jesus stood and cried, saying, If any man thirst let him come to me, and drink.

He that believeth on me, as the scripture hath said, out of his belly (i.e. from the source of his emotions) shall flow rivers of living water.

But he spoke of the Spirit, which they that believed on him were to receive.

Willow branches were a great feature in the temple, where they were placed round the altar, and the priests encircled the altar, palm-branch in hand, singing a verse of the Hallel:

I pray O lord save now! (hoshannah)
I pray O lord give success now!

It was at this feast that Jesus made use also of the theme of light: 'I am the light of the world.' (John VIII.12)
He has just interpreted the Law of Moses in relation to the woman taken in adultery and the story goes on, after further controversy, to relate the healing of the man born blind. Light, a prominent element in the feast, is related to physical and spiritual vision and to the light of truth.

THE FEAST OF HANUKKAH – DEDICATION

The story of the institution of this feast is given in 1 Maccabees IV. 36 to 59. Antiochus Epiphanes had desecrated the temple and the altar, erecting over the altar of holocausts a pagan altar (the 'abomination of desolation') and sacrificed on it swine, to Zeus Olympios, on 25 Kislev (December) 167 B.C. Three years later, the victorious Judas Maccabeus purified the sanctuary, built a new altar and consecrated it on 25 Kislev 164 B.C., the anniversary of its profanation (2 Maccabees. X.5) and decreed that a feast should be observed on this date each year. This was also the date of the dedication of Solomon's temple (1 Kings VIII.2) and also of the altar which was erected after the exile (though the last is related, in Ezra III.4, to the feast of the tabernacles). Tabernacles and Hanukkah are often associated; each lasted eight days and palms were carried on each occasion, but here the

77

resemblance ends. This feast of Hanukkah commemorates all three dedications.

Josephus calls it the Feast of Lights; there are mentions of it only here and there in the Mishnah, it was not popular with the rabbis because of their hatred of the Hasmoneans, but it captured popular imagination, and it is still kept.

It was a most joyful feast. Apart from the sacrifices in the temple, green branches of palm were carried by the people and hymns were sung; the title of Psalm XXX says it was sung 'at the dedication of the house':

> Thou hast turned for me my mourning into dancing; thou hast loosed my sackcloth, and girded me with gladness:

> To the end that my (soul) may sing praise to thee, and not be silent, O LORD my God, I will give thanks unto thee for ever. (verses 11 and 12)

But the principal psalm sung was the Hallel (Psalms CXIII to CXVIII) Psalm CVIII. v 27 doubtless refers to this festival:

> The LORD is God and he hath given us light: bind the sacrifice with cords, even unto the horns of the altar. (Or, as this is sometimes translated;

> 'Bring your processions (or your dance), palms in hand, close to the horns of the altar.')

Lights are the great feature of this feast. In this too it has been compared with the Feast of Tents, but the lights here are quite different; they are kindled at home, near the entrance door opening on to the street (when the inhabitants were threatened with persecution they had to be moved within).

Traditionally a miracle happened at the purification of the temple by Judas Maccabeus. When the time came for the relighting of the 'continual lamp' only a small cruse of consecrated oil could be found, sufficient for one day; but it lasted miraculously until the eighth day when a fresh supply could be prepared.

One light is lit on the first day of the feast, two on the second, until on the eighth day there are eight; the reason for this is not known. It was disputed between Hillel and Shammai whether the order should be one to eight, or eight to one, Hillel supporting

the first Shammai the second: the matter was eventually decided
in favour of Hillel's ruling.

The ceremony was more particularly connected with the home
but also took place in the synagogue. When the Hanukkah light
is kindled the following blessings are chanted by the person who
kindles it and those who see it kindled:

> Blessed art Thou, O Lord our God, King of the Universe, who
> hast sanctified us by thy commandments and commanded us to
> kindle the hanukkah light.

> Blessed art Thou, O Lord our God, King of the universe, who
> didst work miracles for our fathers, in those days at this season.

and, said only on the first night:

> Blessed art Thou, O Lord, King of the universe, who hast let
> us live, and sustained us, and caused us to reach this season.

Then a hymn of praise, extolling God's deliverance is sung.

Hanukkah falls around Christmastime and the lighting of lamps
and candles is natural at this, the darkest time of the year; perhaps
we may compare Hanukkah lights with the lights we hang on our
Christmas trees. Some Christians still observe an old custom of
lighting a candle on Christmas Eve and placing it in the window
onto the street, as a symbolic welcome to Mary and Joseph, who
were seeking shelter in Bethlehem at this time.

No profane use may be made of the Hanukkah lamps and no ordinary work done by their light. Women and girls are encouraged to
kindle Hanukkah lights for themselves. Children share prominently
in the festival and are told stories, given presents, especially on the
first and last days of the festival. the poor are remembered and
begging from door to door, not permitted at other times in Jewish
society, is allowed.

In the synagogue, Hanukkah is marked by two special features.
The Hanukkah light is kindled each evening, followed by the
chanting of Psalm XXX, the psalm for the dedication, just as it
was sung by the Levites in the temple, and in the morning the Hallel
(Psalms CXIII to CXVIII, treated as a single unit) is sung at the
conclusion of the Amidah Prayer. It is possible that the Hallel was
compiled in its present form for this feast, and thence introduced to

the feasts of Passover, Pentecost and Tents. It is treated as a single composition preceded by a special blessing.

There is also a special paragraph in the thanksgiving benediction of the Amidah Prayer:

> We thank Thee also for the miracles

which refers to the Maccabean triumphs, culminating in the re-dedication of the temple.

During the eight days special lessons are read:

> Numbers VII and VIII (giving an account of the gifts which were given at the dedication of the altar of the tabernacle); and

> VIII 1 to 4 (which refer to the kindling of the lights of the holy candlestick);

On the Sabbath occuring within the feast:

> Zechariah IV.1 to 14 (the vision of the golden candlestick) is the prophetic lesson; and

If a second Sabbath occurs during the feast:

> 1 Kings VIII.23 to 53 (the dedication of Solomon's temple).

We see Jesus attending this feast in John X. 22,23):

> And it was the feast of the dedication at Jerusalem: it was winter;

> And Jesus was walking in the temple in Solomon's porch.

It is the occasion of fierce disputes about his messianic claims at the end of which his enemies seek to seize him, but he escapes and withdraws beyond the Jordan, where: 'Many believed on him' (John X.42).

THE FEAST OF PURIM (OR LOTS)

This feast is quite different from Hanukkah; the book of Esther is written to justify it, but this is not an historical book and the feast it seeks to promote is totally different from any of the feasts we have examined. It is not a religious feast, strictly speaking, nor is it held, directly, in honour of the God of Israel, whose name is not even mentioned in the Hebrew Book of Esther. Nor is it connected with the ancient history of the Chosen People. It contains no cultic Hebrew elements and is clearly of foreign origin. Its name seems to come from the Akkadian word *puru* meaning 'lots', but this is not Hebrew and had to be glossed by the Hebrew *gorah* in the background story; Haman had cost lots (*pur*) during Adar to exterminate the Jews and this wicked plot was turned against him and he was hanged:

> In the first month, which is the month Nisan...they cast Pur, that is the Lot, before Haman from day to day, and from month to month, to the twelfth month, which is the month Adar.
>
> (Esther II.7)

This casting of lots would seem to be more suitable to a new year feast, and there is no stress on any such practice in the Jewish feast: it merely gives the feast its name.

The feast probably originated in the cities of the Eastern Diaspora, perhaps in Susa itself, and probably commemorates a pogrom from which the Jews escaped in a way which seemed to them miraculous; perhaps in the fourth century B.C. Ben Sirach, writing about 190 B.C. does not mention Mordecai or Esther in praising Israel's ancestors (Ecclesiasticus XLIV to L). The feast is first mentioned in 2 Maccabees. XV.36 where it is called 'The Day of Mordecai' and is fixed for 14 Adar. The Hebrew text of Esther calls it 'The Days of Purim.' It is next mentioned by Josephus (*Antiquities* XI.vi.13) and so becomes historical; we can only say that it was a popular feast of suspect origin, but that it was accepted by the rabbis is proved by the acceptance of the Book of Esther into the Old Testament Canon. Further, the ritual is described in rabbinic writings. It was preceded by a day of fasting on 13 Adar, and in the evening lamps were lit in all the houses and all went to the synagogue; 14 and 15 Adar were days of rejoicing. Everyone went to the synagogue to listen to the reading of the Book of Esther and while the story was being read the congregation interrupted with curses against Haman and the wicked in general and the meeting closed with the blessing of Mordecai, of Esther and of all Israelites.

The feast was the occasion for the giving of presents and alms, and the pious made gifts with religious intentions. Otherwise the feast was quite secular, taken up with banquets and amusements and considerable liberty was allowed. The rabbis allowed that a man might go on drinking until he could no longer tell the difference between 'Cursed be Haman' and 'Blessed be Mordecai'; this is unique in Judaism; drunkeness is not commonly encouraged in Jewish practice. Later the custom developed of putting on disguises representing the different characters in the story, and the feast became the carnival of the Jewish religion. We may compare it with our Shrove Tuesday, 'Mardi Gras', before the fast of Lent begins and which, in many Latin countries is still kept as a similar type of carnival.

The Book of Esther (IX.28) orders the feast to be kept, but gives no instructions about how this is to be done.

The most important part of the synagogue service is the reading of the book; the entire text is chanted at evening and again at morning prayer. This is done from a parchment scroll, called the *megillah*, not from a printed book; the scroll is specially prepared by Jewish scribes according to certain rules, and the congregation follow in printed books. There is a special blessing before and after the reading.

On the eve of the feast it is customary to have a money collection for the poor. The Book of Esther instructs that the feast shall be one: 'of gladness and feasting, and a good day, and of sending portions one to another, and of gifts to the poor.' (Esther IX.22)

Although certainly kept in New Testament times there is no mention of it there.

It is clear that Jesus was a participant in the rich variety of feasts and festivals of the Jewish faith. His teaching, as we have seen, was coloured by the celebration around him. Christianity has continued this sense of gathering for celebration of the great things God had done for us, to study the Law He has given us, to ask pardon for our failures, and to praise His holy name.

Conclusion

The facile belief, long held among Christians, that the Jews live by law, the Christians by love, dies hard. But the truth is that for both of us the Law is Love:

> What is hateful to thyself, do not do to thy fellow men; this is the whole Torah, the rest is only commentary.
> (Rabbi Hillel, c 10 to 30 A.D.)

> Have we not one father, hath not one God created us?
> (Malachi.II.10. c 460 B.C.)

> ..what doth the LORD require of thee, but to do justly, and to love mercy and to walk humbly..
> (Micah.VI.8. c. 725 B.C.)

Jesus, when asked which was the first and greatest commandment answered:

> The first is, Hear O Israel, the LORD is one:

> And thou shalt love the LORD thy God with all thy mind, and with all thy strength.

> And the second is this, Thou shalt love thy neighbour as thyself. There is none other commandment greater than these.
> (Matthew XII.37 to 40)

and also, like Hillel, whose teaching he doubtless knew, he said:

> All things therefore whatsoever ye would that men should do unto you, even so do ye unto them: for this is the law and the prophets.
> (Matthew.VII.12)

Law is not so much a binding legal restriction as a blue-print for living; there is a law peculiar to each species of created being by which it exists and fulfils the purpose for which God created it:

from the Laws of the Universe, by which the planets move, to the laws of biology by which each seed grows to maturity and reproduces 'after its kind' (Genesis.I.11). The law of God for man is of the same nature, and by obeying it man becomes more truly man: but whereas the stars, the beasts, the vegetable and mineral kingdoms obey Him automatically, to mankind alone He has given the capacity to understand and to obey, or disobey. His law for us is a common heritage developed throughout the millenia of human history; for the Jew it is found in the Bible, especially in the five books of Moses, and in the rabbinic writings. For the Christian it is also found in the Bible, with its addendum in the New Testament.

The Jews believe that the Torah (the Law) was offered by God to all mankind, but only the Hebrews accepted it; Christians believe that Jesus' interpretation of the Law was offered by God to all mankind, but only the Christians accepted it. But in each case the Lord God, blessed be He, accepted man's decision and continued to work out his almighty purpose through his wayward children; it was not He, but these fallible children, who tried to force what they believed to be right on each other, thereby turning good to evil, love to hate.

Now, after nearly twenty centuries of misunderstanding and hatred, we are both faced by a world dominated by violence and materialism, and we can only hope that in the face of it we may grow to see how much we have in common, how much we have to give to each other. Our brethren the Jews are experienced in facing persecution: no other race has suffered as they have. They have remained united, faithful to their witness to God's revelation. Now we are called to live together, by that revelation, in a world where 'the fool' says openly 'There is no God.'

We do not deny our differences, but we remember too that we both believe in the One, True God, the Father, the Creator:

> Hear O Israel, the Lord our God, the Lord is One.

> I believe in One God, the Lord, the Almighty,
> Maker of all things, seen and unseen.

He is Alpha and Omega, the Beginning and the End, Who was, Who is, and Who will be: YAHWEH: ADONAI.

We have, too, one great expectation in common: the coming of God's Kingdom: whether we see our expectations fulfilled in the mythological imagery of the prophets, or prefer to demythologize our dreams, matters not at all. We are probably equally far from any true concept of what God holds in store for his people: how could finite language expect to express a vision of eternity. But we believe that the realization of those dreams will be hastened by our attempts to obey the law of love which He has revealed to us. Then we shall be able to say:

> Justice shall flow down like water,
> And peace like an everlasting stream.
> Mercy and truth are met together;
> Righteousness and peace have kissed each other.
> Truth springeth out of the earth;
> and righteousness has looked down from heaven
>
> (Psalm LXXXV.10)

Now, after all these centuries of cultural conditioning, from Adam to Abraham, from Abraham to Moses, from Moses to Jesus, from Jesus to the present day we are coming to learn that the law of love is a law of toleration, of respect for each individual made in God's image, made to carry out his purpose in the way He directs, not necessarily in the way we think best.

During recent years, many memorable steps have been taken in our journey towards mutual understanding between Christians and Jews. To mention four; on March 4th 1986, Sir Sigmund Steinberg was created a knight of the Papal Order of St. Gregory the Great, on 13th April Pope John Paul II visited the Rome synagogue and in May leaders of earth's major religions met at Assisi and prayed side by side. In the 1988 New Year's Honours List, the Chief Rabbi of England, Sir Immanuel Jacovits, was made a peer. He is noted for his wisdom, tolerance and common sense, and his presence in the House of Lords will no doubt enrich the debates there. In the words of Pope John Paul when he addressed the synagogue in Rome:

> May we go forward together towards the creation of a just and peaceful society, free from every tendency towards racial and religious prejudice, acting as joint trustees of the moral law summarized in the ten commandments.

The Ten Commandments

Thou shalt not make unto thee a graven image, nor the likeness of any form that is in heaven above, or that is in the earth beneath, or that is in the waters under the earth:

Thou shalt not bow down thyself unto them, nor serve them: for I the LORD thy God am a jealous God, visiting the iniquities of the fathers upon the children, unto the third and fourth generation of those that hate me;

And showing mercy unto thousands of them that love me and keep my commandments.

Thou shalt not take the Name of the LORD thy God in vain; for the LORD will not hold him guiltless that taketh his name in vain.

Remember the Sabbath day, to keep it holy.

Six days shalt thou labour and do all thy work:

But the seventh day is a Sabbath unto the LORD thy God: in it thou shalt not do any work, thou, nor thy son, nor thy daughter, thy manservant nor thy maidservant, nor thy cattle, nor thy stranger that is within thy gates.

For in six days the LORD made heaven and earth, the sea, and all that in them is, and rested the seventh day: wherefore the LORD blessed the sabbath day, and hallowed it.

Honour thy father and thy mother: that thy days may be long in the land which the LORD thy God giveth thee.

Thou shalt do no murder.

Thou shalt not commit adultery.

Thou shalt not steal.

Thou shalt not bear false witness against thy neighbour.

Thou shalt not covet thy neighbour's house, thou shalt not covet thy neighbour's wife, nor his manservant, nor his maidservant, nor his ox, nor his ass, nor anything that is thy neighbour's.

(Exodus XX.4ff)

Sources

HISTORICAL

1 Maccabees is a Hebrew translation from a Greek book; it deals with Jewish history from 175 to 135 B.C. Chapters I to XIII were written about 100 B.C.. The date of Chapters XIV to XVI is disputed. The book deals with the reign of John Hyrcanus as High Priest (132 to 104) and seeks to glorify the Hasmoneans.

II Maccabees was written to glorify Jadas Maccabeus. It gives an account of the institution of the feast of Hanukkah, when Judas cleansed and rededicated the temple, which Antiochus IV had desecrated.

Josephus who was born about A.D. 37, was a Jewish historian and is our chief historical source. He belonged successively to the schools of the Pharisees, the Sadducees and the Essenes, but was mostly allied to the Pharisees. He fought against the Romans in the war which culminated in A.D. 70, but in time became their apologist. *The Jewish War* was written in Aramaic and throws a little light on the religion of the Jews around A.D. 80; *The Archaeology of the Jews*, with at least the title in Greek, and *The Jewish Antiquities*, with a Latin title, were completed by A.D. 93 and deal with Jewish history from creation to A.D. 66 (the date of the outbreak of war with Rome). They throw very little light on the inner religion of the Jews and contain a good deal of contradiction and exaggeration.

Others: There are many Greek and Roman historical writers from this period who make 'by the way' references to the Jews, but they contain little or nothing to our purpose.

ARCHAEOLOGICAL

Coins and inscriptions are of interest; we have many from the Seleucidian period from various cities and areas, especially Judea.

Jewish coins bear no human figure, they are decorated with flowers, fruit etc. The coins of Herod the Great have Greek, not Hebrew inscriptions; those of Archelaus have the title 'ethnarch'; and of Herod Antipas 'tetrarch'; those of Herod Agrippa I, however, did have his portrait and were inscribed 'Great King Agrippa Friend of Caesar'. Bronze coins issued by Pontius Pilate bear the name 'Tiberius Caesar' etc.

This last is of interest when we recall the story of Jesus and the coin of tribute:

> Tell us...what thinkest thou? is is lawful to give tribute unto Caesar or not?
>
> But Jesus said...Show me the tribute money, and they brought him a penny.
>
> And he said unto them, Whose image and superscription?
>
> They said unto him Caesar's.
>
> (Matthew XXII. 17 to 19)

In Jesus' time the 'superscription' would doubtless have been Tiberius Caesar's; if Matthew was writing in the Diaspora, possibly Syrian Antioch, he would be used to seeing the emperor's head as well.

The Balustrade Inscription found in the temple ruins reads:

> No alien is to enter within the balustrade and enclosure around the temple. Anyone caught will be liable to the death penalty.

This is reflected in the account in Acts, where the crowd is incited against Paul, who is accused, falsely, of bringing Gentiles into the temple area:

> Crying out, Men of Israel, help: This is the man'...(who) 'brought Greeks into the temple, and has defiled this holy place...
>
> and all the city was moved, and people ran together; and they laid hold on Paul, and dragged him out of the temple; and straight-way the doors were shut.
>
> (Acts XXI. 28 to 30)

Many non-literary papyri give information about the daily life and working of the lower law courts, but they contain nothing to our purpose.

RABBINIC LITERATURE

The Targums are translations of the scriptures from Hebrew to Aramaic and, as translations tend to, sometimes reflect the opinions of the times in which they were made.

The Midrashim are interpretations of the scriptures arranged by biblical books: e.g. Midrash of the Book of Genesis.

The Mishnah contains the teaching of the rabbis and is arranged in topics, e.g. 'Sabbath'. It was known among Jews, including those who formed the early Christian Church, as the oral traditions, and although acknowledged by the Sadducees was not considered by them to be authoritative; many of the gospel disputes turn on the interpretation of these traditions. They were collected and written down at Jamnia, between 175 and 200 A.D. and from then on were regarded as authoritative by all Jews. But they contain the treasured opinions of rabbis and scholars from at least 200 B.C. and are invaluable to us since they reflect religious ideas and practices, forms of worship and pious observances from New Testament times.

THE RELIGIOUS WRITINGS

The Tenach. Central to both Judaism and Christianity is the Bible, known among the Jews as the Tenach, from its three parts, consisting of: The Torah (the five books of Moses: Genesis, Exodus, Leviticus, Numbers, Deuteronomy); the N'bim (the prophets) and the K'tubim (the books of psalms, songs and precepts). By New Testament times The Tenach had come to be recognized as The Book, which demanded study both for general knowledge and for answers to specific questions. But some groups had already begun to study and use it in support of their particular views or interests. For instance Josephus used it to quarry history, with little interest in its religion or theology. The author of IV Ezra was preoccupied with God's justice and with eschatology, he is interested neither in history nor in the laws of Moses, for him the Messiah is central. The author of The Wisdom of Solomon makes the Tenach a plea for the recognition of wisdom-revelation as a sure guide against idolatry. Christian writers, including those who wrote the Gospels, used it to prove their claim that Jesus was God's Messiah. Rabbinic interpretation focused almost entirely on the laws of Moses. And so it has gone on, through the centuries, with many different groups finding justification for their opinions in the sacred text.

THE APOCRYPHA AND PSEUDEPIGRAPHA

These include the *Apocrypha* (books-of doubtful origin, not considered by all authorities to be canonical) and the *Pseudepigrapha* (apocalyptic writings 'to be hidden from all except the wise'). The apocryphal writings are included in the Septuagint, but not in the Hebrew Bible; the pseudepigraphic writings are in neither. Some of these books provide information about synagogual Judaism older than that found in the rabbinic literature; they usually show great concern about describing the future. Most were written between 200 B.C. and A.D. 200.

1 Esdras contains material found in Chronicles XXXV to XXXVI. 23 and Ezra and Nehemiah.

Tobit reflects ancient folklore from the time of the Assyrian exile from Israel (722 B.C.). Tobit, in Nineveh, although a northern Israelite of the tribe of Nephthali, remained loyal to the law, including the food laws and the laws of purity, and helped his fellow exiles in the city of Nineveh. On the feast of Shavuot (Pentecost) he invited poor Jews to take food with him and he found and buried a Jewish corpse, after sunset; then, being ritually defiled, he slept outside. The book is fictional, and Tobit is a portrait of Jewish piety. The laws he obeys are taken from, or inferred from the Bible; he has a wife Anna and a son Tobias, to whom he gives much advice such as is to be found in wisdom literature:

> My son, when I am dead bury me; and despise not thy mother, but honour her all the days of thy life, and do that which shall please her, and grieve her not...

> My son be mindful of the Lord our God all thy days, and let not thy will be set to sin, or to transgress his commandments: do uprightly all thy life long, and follow not the ways of unrighteousness.

For if thou deal truly, they doings shall prosperously succeed
thee, and to all them that live justly

Give alms of thy substance; and when thou givest alms, let not
thine eye be envious, neither turn thy face from any poor, and the
face of God shall not be turned away from thee

(IV. 3ff.)

The book was written perhaps c.200 B.C. and outside Judea.
Fragments have found in the Dead Sea Scrolls. The rising doc-
trine of the resurrection does not appear. Unfortunately there is
no direct information of how the diaspora Jews maintained their
religion, such as information about their synagogues. It stresses the
marriage and family bond within Judaism, almsgiving, abiding by
the dietary laws and abiding trust in God in spite of all adversity;
to enable his faithful to fulfil this trust he will even send an
angel as guide.

Judith is patriotic fiction; scholars vary in dating it any time
between the seventh century B.C. and the second A.D. But the most
likely date would appear to be around 150 B.C. Judith represents the
ideally pious widow living a noble life in conformity with biblical
injunctions.

Additions to the Book of Daniel These are to be found in the
Septuagint but not in the Hebrew Bible. They consist of the following: 1. The prayer of Azariah; this is inserted after Chapter III.23
in the Hebrew Bible. It includes the subjection of the fire by an
angel and the Song of the Three Children: the first implies that the
temple is desecrated, the second that it has been rededicated.2. The
Story of Susannah, a story which celebrates the chastity of a Jewish
matron, even to condemnation, falsely, to death, and the triumph
of ingenuity, shrewdness and wisdom in Daniel, whom God sends
to vindicate her. 3. Bel and the Dragon reflects the scorn in which
Jews held idol worship.

The Letter of Jeremiah This predicts that the exile, in Babylon,
will last for seven generations (Jeremiah XXIXX.10 predicts sev-
enty years.) The letter is an expansion of Jeremiah X.II and was
written just before or during the Maccabean Age. It survives in
Greek only and in a tiny fragment in the Dead Sea Scrolls; its
main theme is a polemic against idols.

The Book of Baruch This is a composite book composed of poetry and prose; it claims to be written in Babylon after the destruction of Jerusalem on 587 B.C. It refers to Nebuchadnessar and his 'son' Belshazzar. Some scholars suggest it belongs to the Maccabean period, others would date it after 70 A.D. The prayer is a confession of sin, in the first person, by the Jerusalem community and the exiles; it ascribes the disaster as due to the neglect of Wisdom, i.e. the divine commandments, but concludes with comfort: God, having punished, will redeem.

The Prayer of Manasseh (Mannasseh was quite the worst of the kings of Judah and to say this was to say something; yet he had the longest reign!) This beautiful prayer was written probably between 200 and 50 B.C. It records that Manasseh, taken prisoner by the Assyrians, repented and was allowed to return to Jerusalem, where he worshipped God faithfully. It is too long to quote here, but a few extracts may give an idea of its quality:

> O Lord, almighty God of our Fathers...who hast made heaven and earth, with all the ornament thereof; who hast bound the sea by the word of thy commandment; who hast shut up the deep, and sealed it by thy terrible and glorious name; ...thou art the most high Lord, of great compassion, longsuffering, very merciful, and repentest of the evils of men; and of thine infinite mercies hast appointed repentance unto sinners, that they may be saved; thou hast appointed repentance to me that am a sinner, for I have sinned above the number of the sands of the sea... I have provoked thy wrath and done evil before thee: I did not thy will nor kept thy commandments, I have set up abominations and I have multiplied offences. Now therefore I bow the knee of mine heart, beseeching thee of grace. I have sinned, O Lord, I have sinned, and I acknowledge mine iniquities; wherefore I humbly beseech thee forgive me O Lord, forgive me and destroy me not with mine iniquities. Be not angry with me for ever,...thou wilt save me, that am unworthy, according to thy great mercy. Therefore I will praise thee for ever all the days of my life: for all the powers of the heavens do praise thee, and thine is the glory for ever and ever. Amen.

This might well be part of the liturgy of the Day of Atonement and could well be adapted in Christian liturgy.

The Wisdom of Solomon This book consists of wisdom sayings in a profound and interesting essay. It has its origin in the Greek

Diaspora and is deeply aware of an alien atmosphere dangerous to Jewish piety and strict morality. Its probable date is around 50 B.C., after Ecclesiasticus but before Philo. There is belief in the after- life, but this is immortality, nor resurrection.

Ecclesiasticus (The Wisdom of Jesus son of Sirach) The book speaks of the high priest Simon, son of Onias, whose dates we know, 219 to 196 B.C., so it is safe to assume it was written towards the end of this time, about 180 B.C. The Greek translation was made by the author's grandson, who came to Egypt around 132 B.C. Some fragments of the original are to found in the Dead Sea Scrolls and it is much quoted in rabbinic literature. The book, although not very exciting, is replete with sound wisdom: piety, obedience to parents, humility, divine rewards and punishments, the practice of self-control and the curbing of passions and lusts; God is merciful, but it is not advisable to rely too much on this. It speaks of duties to friends, wife, servants, animals, children: to God, to priests, to the poor; of the need for prudence when dealing with others.

IV Ezra (also known as II Esdras) This has survived in Latin and other translations, but only a few lines in Greek. It contains Christian additions. The original chapters seem to be III to XIV; it is popularly dated about 100 A.D. and deals partly with the destruction of Jerusalem and the denunciation of Rome (called 'Babylon'). But it is important in that it is an enquiry into how a just God could allow such evils to befall Jerusalem.

The Book of Enoch This book was written in both Hebrew and Aramaic and was well- known to both Jews and Christians; its popularity seems to have waned around the fifth century. It is full of symbolism, extreme partisanship and exaggeration; but it is important in its clear statements about the Messiah and the resurrection, and there is abundant use of the symbol of the Son of Man.

Jubilees (sometimes called 'Little Genesis') reviews Jewish history from Genesis I.i. through Exodus XIV.31. It embroiders by additions and judicious omissions. It is unique in reckoning time by jubilees, i.e. 7 x 7 years, to the fiftieth, the jubilee year. It was originally written in Hebrew or Aramaic, but now survives only in Ethioptic. It sees the Laws as revealed to the Patriarch Abraham before they were revealed to Moses in Exodus XX. Abraham observed the 'mosaic' sacred days: New Year, New Moon, Booths, Passover, Weeks etc. He also observed the Sabbath prohibitions, said grace at meals and celebrated a clear, though undeveloped Passover Seder! There is great scorn of idolatry; angels were his teachers and he spoke Hebrew. (This was Adam's language, but it was forgotten after the Tower of Babel.) Circumcision, as well as the covering of the genitals, a thing ridiculed by the Greeks, was ordained from heaven. Israel and the angels were alone in celebrating the Sabbath and rigid separation from the Gentiles is ordered; there is to be no eating with them nor any fraternization and intermarriage is rigidly prohibited. Angels, good and bad, and demons abound, but ideas about an after-life are not clearly expressed. The book was probably written about 150 to 100 B.C.: fragments have been found at Qumram.

The Dead Sea Scrolls The first of these were accidentally discovered in 1947 in a cave in the Judean Wilderness on the shores of the Dead Sea not far from the ruins of Khirbet Qumran, about eight miles south of Jericho. Khirbet Qumran was the centre of a Jewish sect, possibly composed of Essenes, who lived a communal religious life divorced from the temple worship and from rabbinic Judaism of their time. Some scholars think that John the Baptist may have belonged to this sect as a boy:

> And the child grew, and waxed strong in spirit, and was in the desert till the day of his showing unto Israel.
>
> (Luke I. 80.)

But if so he must have developed a distinctive vocation outside the monastery where he grew up, since the wandering life of preacher and baptizer, a life similar to that of the ancient prophets, was not compatible with the discipline laid down for members of the sect living at Khirbet Qumran, as we know it from the documents which have survived to us.

The first documents found consisted of both biblical and non-biblical scrolls and aroused intense interest among scholars and archaelologists and by 1956 ten more caves, containing scrolls and fragments of scrolls, had been discovered. Some of the documents are biblical, consisting of recensions of the Hebrew Bible from a text different from the Massoretic to which we are accustomed and some very much older than anything which we had before. Others contain apocalyptic writings and yet others are concerned with the beliefs and practices of a Jewish religious sect, presumably that of Qumran. They lay undisturbed for at least two thousand years, and are of unparalleled value to students of Palestinian Judaism in the inter-testamental period. Unfortunately they are of limited relevance to our study. They highlight the religious ferment taking place in Palestine between approximately 150 B.C. and 100 A.D., but they represent the beliefs and practices of a sect which rejected the temple and contemporary rabbinic teaching, and which was unable to adapt to the catastrophe of A.D. 70. Christianity and rabbinic Judaism continued to develop side by side for the next two or three decades, adapting and developing to the needs of the time, the one bending and expanding, the other becoming more rigid and withdrawn; but the perfectionism of Qumran proved unable to adapt and finally perished, along with Jewish Independence, at the gallant defence of Masada in A.D. 73.

Glossary

ABIB	The biblical name of the first month, now called Nisan: March/April
AHABAH	Love: the name of the second blessing said before the recitation of the Shema in the synagogue
ADAR	The twelfth month: February/March
ADAR II	The extra month added in leap year
AFIKOMEN	Dessert: the morsel reserved until the end at the passover seder
ALENU	It is meet for us: the name of a prayer said in the synagogue
AMIDAH	The synagogue prayer also called the eighteen blessings, said in every service
APOCRYPHA	Books of scripture accepted by some but not all as canonical
AV	The fifth month: July/August
BAR	Son
BAR MITZVAH	Son of the Covenant: the ritual in which a thirteen-year-old Jewish boy is received as a full adult member of the congregation
BERAKAH	A blessing, benediction
BETH	House
BOOTHS	Houses built of branches in which Jews live during the Feast of Booths, or Tabernacles, or Succoth

CHEROSETH	A sweet sauce in which the bitter herbs are dipped at the passover seder
CHESRAN	The eighth month: October/November
DIDACHE	The Teaching of the Twelve Apostles: an early second century Christian writing
ELUL	The sixth month: August/September
EMETHWE-YATZIB	True and constant: the title of the first of the two blessings which follow the recitation of the Shema in the Synagogue
ETHROG	The citron carried by the worshippers at the Feast of Tabernacles
ESCHATOLOGY	The doctrine of death, judgment, heaven and hell
FIRSTBORN	The first child of his mother, provided it is a male child; if the first child is female then there can never be a 'firstborn' in that family
GAMALIEL	A first century rabbi, teacher of Paul of Tarsus and a disciple of Rabbi Hillel
GOD-FEARER	A Gentile, attracted to Judaism but who has not as yet fully accepted the Jewish law
GORAH	Lots
GUELLAH	Redemption: alternative title, to that of *emethwe-yatzib*, of the first of the blessings which follow the recitation of the Shema in the synagogue
HAFTARAH	The lesson taken from the prophets, read in both temple and synagogue
HAGGADAH	Telling forth, recitation: used of the telling forth of Israel's history of salvation which takes place in the Passover

	Seder: known as the Passover Haggadah
HALLEL	Psalms CXIII to CXVIII, sung as a single unit at major Jewish feasts in both temple and synagogue
HANUKKAH	Dedication: a Jewish feast held in honour of the rededication of the temple by Judas Maccabeus
HASHKIBENU	Cause us to lie down: the title of the second blessing which follows the recitation of the Shema in the synagogue at evening prayer
HASMONEAN	The name of the kingly house which ruled Judah after the success of the Maccabean revolt
HILLEL	A famous rabbi, contempory of Rabbi Shammai and near-contemporary of Jesus (c. A.D. 10 to 30) known for his gentleness
HOSHANNAH	Save now!
HOSHANNAH RABBA	The Great Hoshannah: a Jewish feast, the culmination of the Feast of Tabernacles
IYAR	The second month: April/May
KIDDUSH	Sanctification
KISLEV	The ninth month: November/December
K'TUBIM	The books of the Hebrew Bible other than those of the Torah and the Prophets
LOTS	Another name for the Feast of Purim
LULAB	A specially prepared palm branch carried by worshippers at the Feast of Tabernacles
MATSOTH	A cake of unleavened bread eaten at passover

MEGILLAH	The scroll of the Book of Esther used by the reader at the Feast of Purim
MESSIAH	The Anointed One
MIDRASH	Interpretation of the Hebrew scriptures
MINIM	Heretics
MISHNAH	The written record of Jewish oral tradition, compiled by the rabbis of Jamnia towards the end of the second century A.D.
MOHAR	The present of money given by a Jewish bride-groom to his father-in-law.
MUSAF	The additional morning service held in the synagogue on feast days
N'BIM	The books of the prophets in the Hebrew Bible
NISAN	The first month: March/April
OMER	A dry measure, about half a gallon
PASCH or PESACH	The Feast of the Passover
PENTATEUCH	The first five books of the Bible (see TORAH)
PENTECOST	The Feast which occurs fifty days after Passover
PHILO	A Jewish philosopher from Alexandria (c. 20 B.C. to c. 40 A.D.)
PROSELYTE	A Gentile who had accepted the full Jewish Law
PSEUDEPIGRAPHA	Secret religious writings; not accepted in the scriptures
PURIM	Lots: The Feast of Esther
RABBI	Teacher: an expert in the interpretation of the Jewish law

ROSH	Head
ROSH CHODESH	Head of the month: i.e. the first day of the month
ROSH HASHANNAH	Head of the year: i.e. New year's Day
SEDER	Order (of service), e.g. The Passover Seder, the service held in the home at the beginning of the feast
SEPTUAGINT	The Greek translation of the Hebrew Bible: usually written LXX
SHAVUOTH	The Feast of Pentecost, or Weeks
SHAMMAI	A famous Jewish rabbi, contemporary of Rabbi Hillel and near-contemporary of Jesus
SHEKINAH	The glory, the presence of God
SHEMA	The 'Hear O Israel...' said by every Jew morning and evening and at the hour of death: said also with blessings before and after in the synagogue
SHEVAT	The eleventh month: January/February
SHILOH	An ancient sanctuary in Israel
SHOFAR	The ram's horn, blown in the synagogue at services on Sabbaths and certain festivals
SILOAM	A pool of water close to the temple, of importance in the temple liturgy especially on the Feast of Succoth
SIMCHAT TORAH	Rejoicing in the Law: a Jewish feast of late institution, not mentioned in the New Testament
SIVAN	The third month: May/June
SUCCOTH	The Feast of Booths, Tents or Tabernacles

TABERNACLES	The Feast of: see Succoth, above
TAMMUZ	The fourth month: June/July
TARGUM	Translation of the Hebrew scriptures with paraphrase and commentary
TENACH	The whole of the Hebrew Bible
TERUAH	Alarm or trumpet blast
TEVET	The tenth month: December/January
TISHRI	The seventh month: September/October
TORAH	The Law, or teaching, contained in the first five books of the Bible: the 'Books of Moses'
TU BISHVAT	The Feast of New Year for Trees
VULGATE	The Latin translation of the Bible, including both the Hebrew and the Christian scriptures
WEEKS	The Feast of Succoth, or Tabernacles
WIDDUY	Confession of sins
YOM	Day
YOM HA'ATZMAUT	Independence Day in Israel
YOM HA DIN	The Day of Judgment
YOM KIPPUR	The Day of Atonement
YOM TERUAH	The Day of the Shofar Blowing
YOM TOV	A festival day
YOM ZIKKARON	The Day of Memorial
YOTSER	Creator: the title of the first of the two benedictions said before the recital of the Shema in the synagogue

101